S0-AXJ-812

Alan L. Ellis, PhD
Ellen D. B. Riggle, PhD

Sexual Identity on the Job: Issues and Services

*Pre-publication
REVIEWS,
COMMENTARIES,
EVALUATIONS . . .*

"**S**exual Identity on the Job: Issues and Services explores the meaning and the lives of lesbian, gay, bisexual, and transgender people in the work place in both theoretical and practical perspectives. It highlights issues being confronted by employers and workers alike. The editors and contributors courageously grapple with dilemmas, and passionately discuss issues ranging in subject matter from multiple cultural and undervalued identities, trends in economic discrimination, economic reasons to provide domestic partner benefits, education needs of decisionmakers, and career concerns as well as career counseling concerns of lesbians, gay, bisexual, and transgender employees.

This thoughful book reveals how discrimination on the job affects the lives of all employees, and provides an exceptional view into the psychological issues faced by lesbian, gay, bisexual, and transgender people related to employment issues."

Ronni L. Sanlo, EdD
Director, Lesbian Gay Bisexual Programs Office, University of Michigan

Sexual Identity on the Job: Issues and Services

ALL HAWORTH BOOKS AND JOURNALS
ARE PRINTED ON CERTIFIED
ACID-FREE PAPER

Sexual Identity on the Job: Issues and Services

Alan L. Ellis, PhD
Ellen D. B. Riggle, PhD
Editors

The Haworth Press, Inc.
New York · London

Sexual Identity on the Job: Issues and Services has also been published as *Journal of Gay & Lesbian Social Services,* Volume 4, Number 4 1996.

© 1996 by The Haworth Press, Inc. All rights reserved. No part of this work may be reproduced or utilized in any form or by any means, electronic or mechanical, including photocopying, microfilm and recording, or by any information storage and retrieval system, without permission in writing from the publisher. Printed in the United States of America.

The development, preparation, and publication of this work has been undertaken with great care. However, the publisher, employees, editors, and agents of The Haworth Press and all imprints of The Haworth Press, Inc., including The Haworth Medical Press and Pharmaceutical Products Press, are not responsible for any errors contained herein or for consequences that may ensue from use of materials or information contained in this work. Opinions expressed by the author(s) are not necessarily those of The Haworth Press, Inc.

The Haworth Press, Inc., 10 Alice Street, Binghamton, NY 13904-1580 USA

Library of Congress Cataloging-in-Publication Data

Sexual identity on the job: issues and services/ Alan L. Ellis, Ellen D. B. Riggle, editors.
     p. cm.
     Includes bibliographical references and index.
     ISBN 1-56024-760-6 -- ISBN 1-56023-076-2 (pbk.)
     1. Gays–Employment–United States. 2. Lesbians–Employment–United States. 3. Bisexuals–Employment–United States. 4. Sexual discrimination in employment–United States. 5. Gender identity–United States. I. Ellis, Alan L., 1957- . II. Riggle, Ellen D. B.

HD6285.5.U6S48 1996   96-20265
331.5–dc20   CIP

INDEXING & ABSTRACTING

Contributions to this publication are selectively indexed or abstracted in print, electronic, online, or CD-ROM version(s) of the reference tools and information services listed below. This list is current as of the copyright date of this publication. See the end of this section for additional notes.

- *AIDS Newsletter c/o CAB International/CAB ACCESS . . . available in print, diskettes updated weekly, and on INTERNET. Providing full bibliographic listings, author affiliation, augmented keyword searching,* CAB International, P.O.Box 100, Wallingford Oxon OX10 8DE, United Kingdom

- *Cambridge Scientific Abstracts, Risk Abstracts,* Environmental Routenet (accessed via INTERNET), 7200 Wisconsin Avenue #601, Bethesda, MD 20814

- *caredata CD: the social and community care database,* National Institute for Social Work, 5 Tavistock Place, London WC1H 9SS, England

- *CNPIEC Reference Guide: Chinese National Directory of Foreign Periodicals,* P.O. Box 88, Beijing, People's Republic of China

- *Digest of Neurology and Psychiatry,* The Institute of Living, 400 Washington Street, Hartford, CT 06106

- *ERIC Clearinghouse on Urban Education (ERIC/CUE),* Teachers College, Columbia University, Box 40, New York, NY 10027

- *Family Life Educator "Abstracts Section,"* ETR Associates, P.O. Box 1830, Santa Cruz, CA 95061-1830

- *Family Studies Database (online and CD/ROM),* Peters Technology Transfer, 306 East Baltimore Pike, 2nd Floor, Media, PA 19063

- *HOMODOK/"Relevant" Bibliographic Database,* Documentation Centre for Gay & Lesbian Studies, University of Amsterdam (selective printed abstracts in "Homologie" and bibliographic computer databases covering cultural, historical, social and political aspects of gay & lesbian topics), c/o HOMODOK-ILGA Archive, O.Z. Achterburgwal 185, NL-1012 DK Amsterdam, The Netherlands

(continued)

- *IBZ International Bibliography of Periodical Literature,* Zeller Verlag GmbH & Co., P.O.B. 1949, d-49009 Osnabruck, Germany

- *Index to Periodical Articles Related to Law,* University of Texas, 727 East 26th Street, Austin, TX 78705

- *INTERNET ACCESS (& additional networks) Bulletin Board for Libraries ("BUBL"), coverage of information resources on INTERNET, JANET, and other networks.*
  - JANET X.29: UK.AC.BATH.BUBL or 00006012101300
  - TELNET: BUBL.BATH.AC.UK or 138.38.32.45 login 'bubl'
  - Gopher: BUBL.BATH.AC.UK (138.32.32.45). Port 7070
  - World Wide Web: http: / / www.bubl.bath.ac.uk./BUBL/ home.html
  - NISSWAIS: telnetniss.ac. uk (for the NISS gateway)
  The Andersonian Library, Curran Building, 101 St. James Road, Glasgow G4 ONS, Scotland

- *Mental Health Abstracts (online through DIALOG),* IFI/Plenum Data Company, 3202 Kirkwood Highway, Wilmington, DE 19808

- *Referativnyi Zhurnal (Abstracts Journal of the Institute of Scientific Information of the Republic of Russia),* The Institute of Scientific Information, Baltijskaja ul., 14, Moscow A-219, Republic of Russia

- *Social Work Abstracts,* National Association of Social Workers, 750 First Street NW, 8th Floor, Washington, DC 20002

- *Sociological Abstracts (SA),* Sociological Abstracts, Inc., P.O. Box 22206, San Diego, CA 92192-0206

- *Studies on Women Abstracts,* Carfax Publishing Company, P.O. Box 25, Abingdon, Oxfordshire OX14 3UE, United Kingdom

- *Violence and Abuse Abstracts: A Review of Current Literature on Interpersonal Violence (VAA),* Sage Publications, Inc., 2455 Teller Road, Newbury Park, CA 91320

(continued)

SPECIAL BIBLIOGRAPHIC NOTES

related to special journal issues (separates)
and indexing/abstracting

☐ indexing/abstracting services in this list will also cover material in any "separate" that is co-published simultaneously with Haworth's special thematic journal issue or DocuSerial. Indexing/abstracting usually covers material at the article/chapter level.

☐ monographic co-editions are intended for either non-subscribers or libraries which intend to purchase a second copy for their circulating collections.

☐ monographic co-editions are reported to all jobbers/wholesalers/approval plans. The source journal is listed as the "series" to assist the prevention of duplicate purchasing in the same manner utilized for books-in-series.

☐ to facilitate user/access services all indexing/abstracting services are encouraged to utilize the co-indexing entry note indicated at the bottom of the first page of each article/chapter/contribution.

☐ this is intended to assist a library user of any reference tool (whether print, electronic, online, or CD-ROM) to locate the monographic version if the library has purchased this version but not a subscription to the source journal.

☐ individual articles/chapters in any Haworth publication are also available through the Haworth Document Delivery Services (HDDS).

ABOUT THE EDITORS

Alan L. Ellis, PhD, is a Research Associate at the Center for Research and Education in Sexuality at San Francisco State University, where he also teaches courses in the Department of Psychology and the Human Sexuality Program. He is a member of the editorial boards of the *Journal of Homosexuality* and the *Journal of Gay & Lesbian Social Services.*

Ellen D. B. Riggle, PhD, is Assistant Professor of Political Science at the University of Kentucky. Her research on the evaluation of political candidates and political tolerance and in the area of gay and lesbian studies has been published in a number of journals, including the *American Journal of Political Science,* the *Journal of Personality and Social Psychology, Political Behavior, American Politics Quarterly,* and the *Journal of Homosexuality.*

Sexual Identity on the Job: Issues and Services

CONTENTS

Foreword

Relentless change is the single constant to be found in the contemporary American workplace. Businesses are increasingly confronted by the demands of responding to global competition, technological reconfiguration and human resource "right-sizing." Clearly, businesses face challenges, risks and opportunities which would have been unimaginable even a few years ago.

Strategies designed to respond to these new demands feature approaches (such as Total Quality Management) that are predicated on the notion of leveraging the unique sets of skills that each employee brings to the workplace. The good news is that this has resulted in broad recognition of the importance of workplace diversity. Every time a person comes into contact with new people, new circumstances, and new perspectives, that person is afforded the means to improve his or her ability to perform effectively on the job.

Valuing diverse perspectives underscores the contributions that each individual makes to the collective enterprise. Being recognized and valued as an important contributor is also a crucial factor in shaping an individual employee's perceptions of self-worth—in the workplace and beyond. Self-realized employees are clearly better able to see the contributions they make to the collective enterprise. As the relevancy of an individual's contribution to the overall collective effort is more easily discerned, the motivation to participate in the collective effort becomes increasingly intrinsic, furthering individual perceptions of value, significance and self-efficacy.

The bad news is that, even though there is broad recognition that

[Haworth co-indexing entry note]: "Foreword." Wagner, Ellen D. Co-published simultaneously in *Journal of Gay & Lesbian Social Services* (The Haworth Press, Inc.) Vol. 4, No. 4, 1996, pp. xiii-xiv; and: *Sexual Identity on the Job: Issues and Services* (ed: Alan L. Ellis, and Ellen D. B. Riggle) The Haworth Press, Inc., 1996, pp. xi-xii; and: *Sexual Identity on the Job: Issues and Services* (ed. Alan L. Ellis, and Ellen D. B. Riggle) Harrington Park Press, an imprint of The Haworth Press, Inc., 1996, pp. xi-xii. Single or multiple copies of this article are available from The Haworth Document Delivery Service [1-800-342-9678, 9:00 a.m. - 5:00 p.m. (EST)].

© 1996 by The Haworth Press, Inc. All rights reserved.

each person must be afforded the means of rising to meet his or her full potential, it is still easier for businesses to articulate this vision than it is to integrate such values within the corporate culture. Gay and lesbian workers routinely experience first-hand the systematized bigotry that arises from ignorance and fear. A number of distracters continue to divert workplace efforts toward diversity and inclusion. For example, domestic partnership benefits may be perceived as costly, and may be avoided because of the perception of increased financial liability. With increased cost being a concrete, tangible concern, a business case can be made with supporting evidence to address the realities rather than the perception of cost so that a change to a company's benefit structure may ultimately be implemented. Other distracters, such as religious biases, homophobia, sexism and racism, represent far more insidious threats to gay and lesbian workers, since these distracters are based more upon bias and ignorance than on tangible substantive evidence.

This special issue is a significant achievement in that it provides gay, lesbian, bisexual, transgendered and straight workers and managers with a compendium of information resources. By providing a focus upon real issues–the past and current status and direction of gay and lesbian workplace concerns; racism, sexism, and homophobia, self-efficacy and self-actualization; domestic partnership issues and workplace productivity–it is increasingly likely that ALL employees, regardless of their sexual orientation, will have the equal opportunity to contribute to the collective enterprise to his or her full potential.

Ellen D. Wagner, PhD
Vice President, Informania, Inc.
Former Professor and Chair
Department of Educational Technology
University of Northern Colorado

Preface

The relationship between an individual's psychological well-being and perceptions of a favorable work environment has been of considerable interest to social science researchers and practitioners for several decades. The psychological benefits of a positive work experience are well documented, as are the detrimental effects of a negative work environment. In light of these costs and benefits, research looking at the specific implications of the relationship between work and the psychological well-being of lesbians, gay men, bisexuals, and transgender individuals has gradually developed and, in the past few years, has seen heightened activity and interest.

We are pleased to contribute to a better understanding of this area with this volume. In the two decades in which research on this topic has developed, a number of issues have remained the same (e.g., concerns regarding disclosure and discrimination) and as the visibility of gay people has increased, a number of other issues have presented themselves (e.g., the possibility of receiving domestic partner benefits). The articles in this volume address both new and relatively older issues relating to ways in which those concerned about the psychological well-being of gay, lesbian, bisexual and transgender workers can address these workers' needs in the workplace, as well as their desire to lead productive and fulfilling lives.

The first article in this volume (Ellis) provides a concise review of literature in this area and its development. Its stated purpose is to chronicle the development of research on this topic, the specific

[Haworth co-indexing entry note]: "Preface." Ellis, Alan L., and Ellen D. B. Riggle. Co-published simultaneously in *Journal of Gay & Lesbian Social Services* (The Haworth Press, Inc.) Vol. 4, No. 4, 1996, pp. xv-xvii: and: *Sexual Identity on the Job: Issues and Services* (ed: Alan L. Ellis, and Ellen D. B. Riggle) The Haworth Press, Inc., 1996, pp. xiii-xv; and: *Sexual Identity on the Job: Issues and Services* (ed: Alan L. Ellis, and Ellen D. B. Riggle) Harrington Park Press, an imprint of The Haworth Press, Inc., 1996, pp. xiii-xv. Single or multiple copies of this article are available from The Haworth Document Delivery Service [1-800-342-9678, 9:00 a.m. - 5:00 p.m. (EST)].

© 1996 by The Haworth Press, Inc. All rights reserved. *xiii* concerns that have been addressed, and where the research currently leaves us. In addition, the review provides some interpretation of past and current research and its implications both for lesbian, gay, bisexual and transgender workers and those (e.g., social service providers) who work with them.

As noted in the review of the literature, much of the early research focused on individuals' personal experiences in the workplace and, often, perceptions and experiences of discrimination. Consistent with the development of the research in this area, the second article in this volume (Rosabal) describes the experiences of those whose queer identity also includes the dynamics of multiple identities resulting from race, gender, and sexual orientation. This article provides those working with lesbian, gay, bisexual, and transgender persons an increased awareness of the psychological demands placed on the individual who is also relating to other cultural, racial, and/or gender concerns and challenges.

Badgett, in the third article in this volume, provides an excellent analysis of current trends in economic discrimination toward lesbians, gay men, and bisexuals in the workplace and the legal situation they face. In addition, she provides social science practitioners and researchers with a solid discussion of the challenges those attempting to document the work experiences of sexual minorities are likely to face (discrimination in various forms including salary, hiring and promotion, and firing).

Next are two articles on specific company actions that social service providers need to be aware of to effectively support their lesbian, gay, bisexual, and transgender clients. Spielman and Winfeld effectively describe the important issues related to domestic partner benefits and provide compelling reasons for offering them. Powers discusses the relationship between feeling included in the organization and productivity. Both of these articles inform social service providers and others about the information necessary to support clients who are concerned about providing health and other benefits to their partners, and about their own effectiveness in the workplace. In addition, these articles assist social service providers in advocating for their clients by providing information that is useful in demonstrating the value of inclusion (both in benefits and in a favorable work environment) to senior management.

The sixth and final article in this volume provides the latest update on career concerns and career counseling of lesbians, gays, bisexuals, and transgender persons. In this article, Pope discusses the dramatic increase in research in this area and the implications of the research findings both for the client and for those who offer career services.

The articles in the volume address a diverse set of issues for lesbians, gay men, bisexuals and transgender individuals in the workplace. However, they share a desire to promote a workplace that offers inclusion, safety, and a place to thrive psychologically and emotionally to all workers. As noted by Powers in his article, ". . . organizations that exclude *any* group from their diversity policies and practices do a huge disservice to the credibility of their entire diversity program." The inclusion through policies of non-discrimination, availability of domestic partner benefits, and solid efforts to eliminate discrimination toward lesbians, gays, bisexuals, and transgender individuals helps create a psychologically favorable environment for all workers.

The co-editors and contributors to this volume have made a special effort to acknowledge the experiences of gay men, lesbians, bisexuals and transgender individuals. However, it is important to remember that the experiences faced by members of each of these groups are distinct. Hopefully, where the distinct challenges faced by members of the separate groups are not discussed, there is recognition of the applicability of the information to all of the groups of individuals. Likewise, although different authors use different terminology, from "sexual minorities" to simply "gays," the information has applicability to all workers.

We would like to extend our thanks to all of the contributors for their efforts in making this volume diverse and dynamic. Also, we would like to thank Raymond M. Berger for his helpful comments. Finally, we extend our gracious thanks to Barry Tadlock and Mitzi Johnson for their assistance and support.

Alan L. Ellis, PhD
Ellen D. B. Riggle, PhD

Sexual Identity Issues in the Workplace: Past and Present

Alan L. Ellis

SUMMARY. The rapidly developing research looking at gay, lesbian, bisexual, and transgender issues in the workplace is reviewed. Research addressing these issues first appeared in the early 1970s and was relatively dormant for several years as researchers focused their attention on the more immediate and compelling concerns of AIDS. In the past few years, however, the number of articles and studies on gay, lesbian, bisexual, and transgender workplace issues has increased greatly as researchers and social service providers have acknowledged this critical aspect of life–employment–and associated issues. The purpose of this article is to chronicle the development of research in this area, the specific concerns that have been addressed, where the research leaves us as we prepare to increase our understanding of these issues, and how they affect the emotional and psychological well-being of lesbian, gay, bisexual, and transgender individuals. *[Article copies available from The Haworth Document Delivery Service: 1-800-342-9678.]*

In Fall 1974, a small bi-monthly journal entitled *Workforce*, published by an Oakland based collective known as *Vocations for Social Change*, devoted an issue to the concerns of gay workers. Although it is not surprising that several of the first articles on lesbian and gay issues in

Alan L. Ellis, PhD, is a Research Associate at the Center for Research and Education in Sexuality (CERES), Department of Psychology, San Francisco State University, San Francisco, CA 94132.

[Haworth co-indexing entry note]: "Sexual Identity Issues in the Workplace: Past and Present." Ellis, Alan L. Co-published simultaneously in *Journal of Gay & Lesbian Social Services* (The Haworth Press, Inc.) Vol. 4, No. 4, 1996, pp. 1-16; and: *Sexual Identity on the Job: Issues and Services* (ed: Alan L. Ellis, and Ellen D. B. Riggle) The Haworth Press, Inc., 1996, pp. 1-16; and: *Sexual Identity on the Job: Issues and Services* (ed: Alan L. Ellis, and Ellen D. B. Riggle) Harrington Park Press, an imprint of The Haworth Press, Inc., 1996, pp. 1-16. Single or multiple copies of this article are available from The Haworth Document Delivery Service [1-800-342-9678, 9:00 a.m. - 5:00 p.m. (EST)].

© 1996 by The Haworth Press, Inc. All rights reserved.

the workplace appeared in a self-defined radical leftist publication, it is surprising (and somewhat disappointing) that, although more than twenty years have passed, the concerns of lesbians, gay men, bisexuals, and transgender workers remain largely the same.[1]

The articles presented in *Workforce* offered written accounts of the difficulties faced by gay workers in coming out of the closet and described many of the fears associated with disclosure of one's sexual identity in the workplace. Twenty years later, these same concerns and fears, and how to address the personal and psychological costs of either remaining in the closet or coming out at work, remain as the primary focus of lesbian, gay, bisexual and transgender workers and those who provide psychological support to them (Elliott, 1993; Williamson, 1993).

Since 1974, research and applied efforts considering sexual identity issues in the workplace can be seen as related directly to the above concerns. For example, the degree to which an individual feels safe about acknowledging his or her sexual identity to coworkers and actual or potential employers is both related to the psychosocial aspects of this issue and is affected by policy and legal actions. Successful efforts to include sexual orientation in non-discrimination statements and job-related legislation provide legal and psychological benefits to those whose sexual identities are other than heterosexual.[2] The purpose of this article is to provide both those who offer counseling and psychological support to lesbian, gay, bisexual and transgender individuals and those whose efforts are of a legal or policy focus, a fairly complete (although not exhaustive) and concise review of the research literature on sexual identity issues in the workplace. In addition, this article provides interpretation of past and current research and its implications for lesbian, gay, bisexual and transgender workers and those who provide social services to them.

THE EARLIEST STUDIES: PERSONAL ACCOUNTS AND REPORTS OF DISCRIMINATION

Many of the earliest articles addressing sexual identity issues in the workplace documented personal accounts and individual struggles toward a sense of freedom and affirmation in the workplace. In one such account, Innes and Waldron (1974) stated, "[we] decided it was time to stop hiding, pretending, and playing the game and to start doing something constructive about [our] own liberation" (p. 28). These personal accounts often spoke of the challenges and perceptions of discrimination that the authors experienced whether in or out of the closet (see Powers, 1993, and Woods, 1993, for more recent personal accounts on being gay in the workplace).

In 1978, Bell and Weinberg added to the research by looking at how stereotypes of homosexuals relate to the workplace experience of gays and lesbians. They noted that, to the degree individuals equate homosexuality with emotional instability, it might be assumed that lesbians and gay men would be likely to have unstable job histories (a basis for discriminating against lesbians and gay men in employment). Bell and Weinberg's findings indicated that gay men's job stability did not differ significantly from that of heterosexuals nor did they differ with respect to job satisfaction. Indeed, they found gay men to be more satisfied with their work than heterosexual men. They did find that lesbians reported more job changes than heterosexual women but found no significant differences in job satisfaction among the lesbian and heterosexual women. Overall, Bell and Weinberg's findings suggested that stereotypes attributing job instability and dissatisfaction to homosexuals were inaccurate. They did find, however, that a number of gay men and women expressed considerable fear and anxiety that disclosure of their sexuality could lead to loss of job or other forms of discrimination.

Concerns about discrimination were evident in much of the early academic writing on workplace issues which focused on reports and perceptions of discrimination against gay men (Escoffier, 1975; Levine, 1979) and lesbians (Levine & Leonard, 1984) in the workplace. As evidence of discrimination was established, a strong justification for additional research looking at the specific psychological and economic impact of such discrimination was established (Levine, 1979). In addition, these studies would later be used to support the need to offer psychological support and to develop policies that deal with the individual and societal costs of such discrimination (McAnulty, 1993).

Sadly, the need to document physical, economic, and psychological discrimination towards lesbian, gay, bisexual and transgender individuals either in or out of the workplace has not decreased over the past twenty years. Indeed, recent surveys suggest that physical violence toward lesbian, gay, bisexual and transgender persons is increasing (see Herek & Berrill, 1992 for an unsettling depiction of current trends in discrimination). In part, as a result of the documentation of increased violence and discrimination, the past two decades have seen a significant increase in the number of private and public institutions that have modified their discrimination clauses to prohibit discrimination based on sexual orientation (Hedgpeth, 1979/1980; Lee & Brown, 1993).

In 1974, *Workforce* reported that only nine cities across the country had a sexual orientation clause in their non-discrimination statements. As of 1993, more than 100 cities and counties had such clauses and eight states prohibited discrimination based on sexual orientation in employment (National Gay and Lesbian Task Force Policy Institute, 1993). In addition to state and municipal protection, a 1993 survey of the Fortune 1000 companies found that more than 70 had a non-discrimination policy that specifically included sexual orientation (National Gay and Lesbian Task Force Policy Institute, 1993). Although these numbers indicate that the majority of states, municipalities, and corporations do not explicitly include sexual orientation in their non-discrimination clauses, they do show a dramatic increase over the past twenty years. Both the early research and the ongoing research documenting real and perceived discrimination have been cited and have been beneficial in altering workplace policies and in passing job-related legislation (i.e., Shevock, Hicks, Campbell, Sandbrook, Garcia, & Rodieck, 1992).

COMING OUT IN THE WORKPLACE

Beginning in the 1980s, a number of academic and research articles considered the psychological, social, and personal implications of coming out in the workplace. No other issue is more compelling and personally involving for those with a sexual identity other than heterosexual, than the choice to come out both in and out of the workplace. Elliott (1993) describes the choice to "pass" or not to "pass"–in other words, whether or not to come out–as the "first decision" to be made by lesbians and gay men in the work-place.

Given the potential psychological and physical consequences of the choice to "come out," the developmental issues associated with, and the process of coming out, have been the subject of considerable research and theoretical focus. In the most cited model on development of a lesbian or gay identity, Cass (1979) describes a process that begins with identity confusion and culminates in identi-ty synthesis. Within this model, identity pride and synthesis–the final stages of the process–involve addressing integration of one's sexual identity in all areas of one's life, including work. Using Cass's model as a foundation, a number of articles have helped define the important psychological and personal concerns that relate specifically to coming out in the workplace, both for lesbians (Hall, 1986; Schneider, 1986) and gay men (Kronenberger, 1991; also see Pope, this volume, for a review of this work).

As noted by Kitzinger (1991), "concealment of homosexuality is rooted in fear of ostracism, taunts, violence, discrimination, harass-ment and the loss of jobs" (p. 225). As noted in the previous discussion on discrimination, there is strong evidence of bigotry, oppression and other examples of external oppression (e.g., Herek & Berrill, 1992). The resulting perception of an unsafe environment both in and outside the workplace leads many l/g/b/t individuals to actively choose not to "come out." A number of articles strongly indicate the need for those working with and desiring to support lesbian, gay, bisexual and transgender persons to be sensitive to these fears and their basis in reality (Buhrke, 1989; Buhrke & Douce, 1991; Elliott, 1993).

In coming to terms with one's sexual identity in the workplace, Gonsiorek (1993) points out that another concern facing lesbians and gay men is the effect of internalized homophobia on career development and choice. As a result of internalized homophobia, lesbians and gay men may sabotage their own lives and "abandon career or educational goals with the excuse that external bigotry will keep them from their objectives" (p. 248). Gonsiorek notes that gay and lesbian individuals will undoubtedly be met with bigotry in the workplace and have one of two options in responding. They may respond in a self-affirming manner, either behaviorally or symbolically or, by not responding, accept second-class status and a view of themselves as inferior. The issue of how a worker responds to his or her own internalized homophobia and to overt examples of bigotry is critical in defining the psychological experience she or he has in the workplace.

Gonsiorek's focus on the possibility of symbolic responses to overt bigotry is worthy of additional development because it can provide lesbian, gay, bisexual and transgender workers with tools to psychologically process incidents of bigotry in a self-affirming and healthy way when a direct behavioral response is unavailable or inappropriate. In addition, the awareness of symbolic responses offers social service providers an avenue to explore with lesbian, gay, bisexual and transgender workers who, for whatever personal and external reasons, choose to remain in the closet but wish to develop self-affirming attitudes.

A number of recent articles have focused on the special concerns of those dealing with multiple minority identities both in and out of the workplace. For example, Espin (1987) discussed a number of developmental models in an effort to describe the psychological processes of individuals who must integrate multiple minority identities as part of their process of coming out. In focusing specifically on the workplace, Rosabal (this volume) addresses the concerns of those integrating gender and racial and ethnic minority identities with their sexual identity. Additional accounts by Gock (1985) and Morales (1983) describe the psychological processes that relate to individuals who face the task of integrating racial, ethnic, and sexual identities.

As noted previously, no other process is more compelling and psychologically involving than the "coming out" process. Gonsiorek (1993) has stated that the coming out process "is an additional developmental event in the lives of lesbian and gay individuals, superimposed on whatever psychological and developmental processes are particular to the individual" (p. 248). In light of this, the ability of those working with lesbian and gay individuals to support and help facilitate the individual's coming out process is critical. Gonsiorek (1993) and Sussal (1994) provide a number of excellent case examples of workplace dilemmas that may affect lesbian and gay employees that are an invaluable tool for assisting those who work with them to better understand the psychosocial concerns associated with and the reality of both external and internal oppression.

CAREER DECISIONS AND DEVELOPMENT

Whether one is heterosexual, bisexual, transsexual, or gay or lesbian, the issues surrounding career choices and development are of critical importance in how we define ourselves and the satisfaction we receive from our lives. It has been suggested that the single greatest predictor of longevity is job satisfaction (*Work in America*, 1973), and career issues for those of any sexual identity present some of the most rewarding and difficult choices of life.

For those whose sexual identities are other than heterosexual, these choices are often affected by considerations related to one's sexual identity. Attempts to understand the relation between sexual identity issues and career choices and development have yielded a number of interesting findings and suggestions for working with lesbian, gay, bisexual and transgender employees. Indeed, the impact of sexual identity on career development and counseling has received greater attention than any other area addressing workplace issues and sexual identity (Pope, this volume; Elliott, 1993; Hetherington, Hillerbrand, & Etringer, 1989; Hetherington & Orzek, 1989). The reader is referred to these articles for a larger discussion of the research findings in this area. For the purposes of this review, recent work considering the link between sexual identity issues and occupational choice and job satisfaction will be discussed as examples of current areas of research that are in a developing stage.

The link between specific occupational choice and sexual identity is of both theoretical and practical interest and has been the subject of a number of studies. At this point, the relation between sexual identity and job choice remains unclear. An equal number of articles support such a link (e.g., Whitam & Dizon, 1979; Whitam & Mathy, 1986) or refute it (e.g., Murray, 1991; Neuringer, 1989), and the degree to which a relation exists, and the potential usefulness of understanding such a relation in working with lesbian and gay workers, is dependent on future research. Even so, there is evidence that sexual identity is related to certain aspects of career development and choice. For example, researchers focusing on the career choices of gay men and lesbians found that uncertainty about career choice among college students was higher for gay men and lower for lesbians than for heterosexual men and women. In addition, they found that heterosexual women and gay men expressed the highest levels of dissatisfaction related to job choice (Etringer, Hillerbrand, & Hetherington, 1990).

In light of research suggesting that satisfied workers live longer (*Working in America*, 1973) the relationship between sexual identity and job satisfaction is another potentially rich and important area for future exploration. An important aspect of job satisfaction is how satisfied an individual is with his or her coworkers (Smith, Hulin, & Crandell, 1969). In a recent study, Ellis and Riggle (forthcoming) found that gay men and lesbians who were out to the majority of their coworkers and their bosses were more satisfied with the relationships they had with their coworkers than those who had not come out. This study was correlational in nature and, as a result, it remains to be determined whether satisfaction with coworkers results from being out or whether it leads to a greater likelihood of coming out. In either case, the results indicate that there is some relationship between being out in the workplace and job satisfaction.

ATTITUDES TOWARDS GAYS AND LESBIANS IN THE WORKPLACE

A few studies have looked at the attitudes of heterosexuals toward gay, lesbian, and bisexual individuals and how these attitudes affect working relationships and work-related activities such as employment interviews. For example, Ellis and Vasseur (1992) found that individuals with negative attitudes towards lesbians and gay men were slightly more likely to choose questions in an interview that focused on the negative qualities of the interviewee than those with more positive attitudes. And, Riggle and Ellis (1993) found that although the respondents to their questionnaire strongly favored employment protections for all people, the application of this general principle of democracy to gays and lesbians was less strongly supported. Even so, recent polls show that the American public supports equal employment rights for gay men and lesbians more strongly than a number of other rights, such as marriage. Sixty-two percent of Americans favor the passage of laws to protect homosexuals against job discrimination whereas only thirty-one percent favor legal recognition of gay marriages (Time/CNN Poll, June 1994).

Specific Occupations/Cases

As the basic foundation of knowledge regarding sexual identity issues in the workplace increases, the concerns and issues of lesbian, gay, bisexual and transgender people in specific occupations or life stages are being addressed. For example, the unique concerns of gay people who require government security clearances and the inappropriate reasons for denial of such clearances based on inaccurate stereotypes were addressed by Herek in 1990. Although the topic of many of these articles is specific to gays and lesbians, general issues such as the reliability and trustworthiness of gay people relative to heterosexuals are relevant to a number of situations. Herek provides evidence that lesbians and gay men are no more likely to have a personality disorder or other evidence of psychological instability, are not more likely to be susceptible to blackmail, or are any less willing to uphold and respect laws and regulations than heterosexuals.

The negative nature of the stereotypes used to deny lesbians and gay men security clearances requires researchers and others to document the inaccuracy of such stereotypes in addressing these concerns. And, although these issues relate specifically to concerns about security clearances, they also focus on stereotyped beliefs that falsely suggest that gay men and lesbians are somehow less trustworthy or capable in the workplace than their heterosexual counterparts. Herek's work and that of others (see Gonsiorek, 1982, for a summary of this research) clearly indicate that sexual identity, per se, is not negatively related to an individual's trustworthiness and/or psychological well-being. Indeed, Herek speculates that because of gay men and women's awareness of how disclosure of an individual's sexual identity may influence their workplace experience, they may tend to be even more trustworthy and less likely to divulge private or classified information.

In addition to focusing on governmental policy regarding gay women and men and security clearances, Herek (1991) and others (Anderson & Smith, 1993) have also addressed the U.S. military's policy regarding homosexuals and found it to be detrimental (both for gays and the military) and unwarranted based on the research. In other areas of employment, articles have focused on gay and lesbian educators (Griffin, 1992; Sears, J. T., 1992; see Fassinger, 1993 for a solid review of the literature on gay and lesbian educators); athletes (Barrett, 1993); and older gay and lesbian employees (Lee, 1993). Savin-Williams (1993) and a series of articles in Harbeck (1992) provide reflections and personal accounts of coming out in the academic workplace and/or classroom.

Many of the issues discussed in these articles have relevance to the general life adjustment of lesbian and gay individuals. For example, a number of the recommendations provided by Fassinger (1993) for "individual, systemic, and societal action that might be taken to improve the experience of lesbian and gay people in education" (p. 137) are also valuable for a number of other occupations. Fassinger speaks to the issues an individual should consider when choosing a location for work, such as size of the community and the current visibility of gay and lesbian issues, as well as the political climate. She also focuses on the importance of raising the awareness of administrators and others about homosexuality, and she speaks to the importance of broad societal changes, such as the repeal of sodomy laws, in improving the atmosphere for lesbians and gay men in education. These issues are of relevance to lesbian, gay, bisexual and transgender workers in almost any occupation.

POLICY ISSUES AND DOMESTIC PARTNER BENEFITS

A number of articles have focused on the issue of corporate, governmental, and institutional policies regarding sexual orientation (Badgett, this volume). As noted earlier, the work of Herek (1990) and others has focused on governmental policies regarding security clearances and participation in the U.S. military. More recently, as part of the development of institutional policies, the inclusion of partners of non-married couples and the concept of domestic partner benefits have been addressed in the private and public sectors (see Spielman and Winfeld, this volume, for an analysis of this area). In addition, the legal rights of lesbian, gay and transgender individuals as determined by organizational policies and federal, state, and local legislation have been addressed by groups such as the Lambda Legal Defense and Education Fund and the American Civil Liberties Union (e.g., Hunter et al., 1992; Wolfson, 1994).

Consulting on Sexual Identity Issues in the Workplace

One of the more recent entries into the research on sexual identity issues in the workplace is in the area of consulting. Two publications deal specifically with the experience of their authors on how to effectively manage sexual identity issues in the workplace (McNaught, 1993; Powers & Ellis, 1995). Both of these publications provide practitioners with useful tools and concepts for working with managers and other employees in addressing the concerns of heterosexuals and their lesbian, gay, bisexual and transgender coworkers. In addition to relying on personal observation and experience in the corporate world, Powers and Ellis (1995) draw from the research on human performance technology and focus on providing managers with the knowledge, skills, tools, and resources to effectively address l/g/b/t concerns (see Powers, this volume). In his book, McNaught (1993) provides several examples of training exercises that may be used to enhance the skills of managers and others working with lesbian and gay individuals.

AIDS in the Workplace

As noted earlier, the attention of a number of researchers during the 1980s was directed toward the psychosocial implications of AIDS, primarily on gay and bisexual men. In some cases this research focused on issues related to the workplace and the reader is encouraged to look at the book by Huber (1992) entitled *AIDS in the Workplace* for a review of this literature.

SOCIAL PSYCHOLOGICAL ISSUES AND CONCLUSION

An underlying argument of this article is that almost all research and applied efforts focusing on sexual identity and the workplace are related to the social and psychological factors that affect lesbian, gay, bisexual and transgender persons in the workplace. For example, research focusing on domestic partnership benefits can be equally important in helping to establish a favorable psychological environment for individuals as research focusing on addressing the psychosocial concerns related to coming out in the workplace. As a result, a familiarity with and awareness of the multiple issues surrounding sexual identity in the workplace are essential in offering lesbian, gay, bisexual and transgender workers both psychological and policy support.

The creation of a favorable workplace environment through a better understanding of the impact of sexual identity issues on workplace issues is the goal of most applications of both theoretical and applied research. A basic tenet of current theories of job motivation, involvement, and productivity is that all workers should be treated with respect and fairness. To the degree that workers are so treated they are more likely to work in ways that support themselves, their coworkers, and their organizations. Continued research and applied efforts to understand and meet the concerns and needs of lesbian, gay, bisexual and transgender workers are an important component of a system that offers both respect and equality to these workers.

NOTES

1. Although the majority of the research discussed in this review deals primarily with lesbian and gay workers, it is hoped that the inclusion of bisexual and transgender individuals will help broaden the overall discussion to one of issues of sexual identity in the workplace. In many cases, the research findings for gay men and lesbians are relevant to others whose sexual identity is not that of the majority (heterosexual). However, in the same way that gay men and lesbians have specific concerns that differ from each other, bisexuals and transgender individuals have concerns that relate specifically to them and research efforts to address those issues are to be encouraged.

2. The use of the term other-than-heterosexual is used both as a brief term to describe lesbians, gay men, bisexuals, and transsexuals; and to acknowledge what Kitzinger (1991) denotes as the heterosexual assumption–the assumption that everyone is heterosexual. As noted by Kitzinger, lesbians and gay men often experience themselves as "outsiders" or "aliens" as a result of the heterosexual assumption. It should be noted that very little of the research to date has specifically considered the issues of bisexuals and transsexuals (although see Earnshaw, 1991, for an exception to this).

REFERENCES

Anderson, C. W., & Smith, H. R. (1993). Stigma and honor: Gay, lesbian and bisexual people in the U.S. military. In L. Diamant (Ed.), *Homosexual issues in the workplace* (pp. 65-89). New York: Taylor & Francis.

Badgett, L. (this volume). Employment and sexual orientation: Disclosure and discrimination in the workplace. *Journal of Gay & Lesbian Social Services.*

Barrett, R. L. (1993). The homosexual athlete. In L. Diamant (Ed.), *Homosexual issues in the workplace* (pp. 161-170). New York: Taylor & Francis.

Bell, A. P., & Weinberg, M. S. (1978). *Homosexualities: A study of diversity among men and women.* New York: Simon and Schuster.

Buhrke, R. A. (1989). Incorporating lesbian and gay issues into counselor training: A resource guide. *Journal of Counseling and Development, 68,* 77-80.

Buhrke, R. A., & Douce, L. (1991). Training issues for counseling psychologists in working with lesbian women and gay men. *The Counseling Psychologist, 19(2),* 216-234.

Cass, V. C. (1979). Homosexual identity formation: A theoretical model. *Journal of Homosexuality, 9,* 219-235.

Earnshaw, J. (1991). Homosexuals and transsexuals at work: Legal issues. In M. J. Davidson & J. Earnshaw (Eds.), *Vulnerable workers: Psychosocial and legal issues* (pp. 241-257). Chichester, England: John Wiley & Sons.

Elliott, J. E. (1993). Lesbian and gay concerns in career development. In L. Diamant (Ed.), *Homosexual issues in the workplace* (pp. 25-43). New York: Taylor & Francis.

Ellis, A. L., & Riggle, E. D. (forthcoming). The relation of job satisfaction and degree of openness about one's sexual orientation for lesbians and gay men. *Journal of Homosexuality.*

Ellis, A. L., & Vasseur, R. B. (1993). Prior interpersonal contact with and attitudes towards homosexuals in an interviewing context. *Journal of Homosexuality, 25(4),* 31-46.

Escoffier, J. (1975). Stigmas, work environment, and economic discrimination against homosexuals. *Homosexual Counseling Journal, 2,* 8-17.

Espin, O. M. (1987). Issues of identity in the psychology of Latina lesbians. In Boston Lesbian Psychologies Collective (Eds.), *Lesbian psychologies: explorations and challenges* (pp. 35-51). Urbana, IL: University of Illinois Press.

Etringer, B. D., Hillerbrand, E., & Hetherington, C. (1990). The influence of sexual orientation on career decision-making: A research note. *Journal of Homosexuality, 19(4),* 103-111.

Fassinger, R. E. (1993). And gladly teach: Lesbian and gay issues in education. In L. Diamant (Ed.), *Homosexual issues in the workplace* (pp 119-142). New York: Taylor & Francis.

Gay workers out of the closets. (1974). *Workforce, 42.*

Gock, T. S. (1985). *Psychotherapy with Asian/Pacific gay men: Psychological issues, treatment approaches, and therapeutic guidelines.* Paper presented at the American Psychological Association Convention, Los Angeles, CA.

Gonsiorek, J. C. (1982). Results of psychological testing on homosexual populations. *American Behavioral Scientist, 25*, 385-396.

Gonsiorek, J. C. (1993). Threat, stress, and adjustment: Mental health and the workplace for gay and lesbian individuals. In L. Diamant (Ed.), *Homosexual issues in the workplace* (pp. 243-264). New York: Taylor & Francis.

Gonsiorek, J. C., & Rudolph, J. R. (1991). Homosexual identity: Coming out and other developmental events. In J. C. Gonsiorek & J. D. Weinrich (Eds.), *Homosexuality: Research implications for public policy*. Newbury Park, CA: Sage.

Griffin, P. (1992). From hiding out to coming out: Empowering lesbian and gay educators. In K. Harbeck (Ed.), *Coming out of the classroom closet* (pp. 167-196). Binghamton, NY: Harrington Park Press.

Hall, M. (1986). The lesbian corporate experience. *Journal of Homosexuality, 16*, 59-75.

Harbeck, K. (Ed.), (1992). *Coming out of the classroom closet*. Binghamton, NY: Harrington Park Press.

Hedgpeth, J. M. (1979/1980). Employment discrimination law and the rights of gay persons. *Journal of Homosexuality, 5*, 67-78.

Herek, G. M. (1990). Gay people and government security clearances: A social science perspective. *American Psychologist, 45*, 1035-1042.

Herek, G. M. (1991). *Is homosexuality compatible with military service? A review of the social science data*. Symposium conducted at American Psychological Association Convention, San Francisco.

Herek, G. M., & Berrill, K. (1992). *Hate crimes*. Beverly Hills: Sage.

Hetherington, C., Hillerbrand, E., & Etringer, B. (1989). Career counseling with gay men: Issues and recommendations for research. *Journal of Counseling and Development, 67*, 452-454.

Hetherington, C., & Orzek, A. (1989). Career counseling and life planning with lesbian women. *Journal of Counseling and Development, 68*, 52-57.

Huber, J. T. (1993). *AIDS in the workplace*. New York: Lexington.

Hunter, N. D. (1992). *The rights of lesbians and gay men: The basic ACLU guide to a gay person's rights*. New York: New Press.

Innes, C., & Waldron, D. (1974). Staying gay, proud . . . and healthy. *Workforce, 42*, 29-32.

Kitzinger, C. (1991). Lesbians and gay men in the workplace: Psychosocial issues. In M. J. Davidson & J. Earnshaw (Eds.), *Vulnerable workers: Psychosocial and legal issues* (pp. 223-240). Chichester, England: John Wiley & Sons.

Kronenberger, G. (1991). Out of the closet. *Personnel Journal, 70*, 40-44.

Lee, J. A., & Brown, R. G. (1993). Hiring, firing, and promoting. In L. Diamant (Ed.), *Homosexual issues in the workplace* (pp. 45-62). New York: Taylor & Francis.

Levine, M. P. (1979). Employment discrimination against gay men. *International Review of Modern Sociology, 9*, 151-163.

Levine, M. P., & Leonard, R. (1984). Discrimination against lesbians in the work force. *Signs: Journal of Women in Culture and Society, 9*, 700-710.

McAnulty, R. D. (1993). The helping professions: Attitudes toward homosexuality. In L. Diamant (Ed.), *Homosexual issues in the workplace* (pp. 105-118). New York: Taylor & Francis.

McNaught, B. (1993). *Gay issues in the workplace.* New York: St. Martin's Press.

Morales, E. (1983). *Third world gays and lesbians: A process of multiple identities.* Paper presented at the American Psychological Association, Anaheim, CA.

Murray, S. O. (1991). "Homosexual occupations" in Mesoamerica? *Journal of Homosexuality, 21,* 57-65.

National Gay and Lesbian Task Force Policy Institute (1991). *Lesbian and gay civil rights in America.* Washington, DC: National Gay and Lesbian Task Force.

National Gay and Lesbian Task Force Policy Institute (1993). *Workplace project preliminary survey of the Fortune 1000 companies on issues of importance to gays, lesbians, and bisexuals.* Washington, DC: National Gay and Lesbian Task Force.

Neuringer, O. (1989). On the question of homosexuality in actors. *Archives of Sexual Behavior, 18,* 523-529.

Pope, M. (this volume). Gay and lesbian career counseling: Special career counseling issues. *Journal of Gay & Lesbian Social Services.*

Powers, B. (1993). What it's like to be gay in the workplace. *Performance and Instruction, 32,* 10-14.

Powers, B. (this volume). The impact of gay, lesbian and bisexual workplace issues on productivity. *Journal of Gay & Lesbian Social Services.*

Powers, B., & Ellis, A. L. (1995). A manager's guide to sexual orientation in the workplace. New York: Routledge.

Riggle, E. D., & Ellis, A. L. (1994). Political tolerance of homosexuals: The role of group attitudes and legal principles. *Journal of Homosexuality, 26,* 135-148.

Rosabal, G. S. (this volume). Multicultural existence in the workplace: Including how I survive as a Latina lesbian feminist. *Journal of Gay & Lesbian Social Services.*

Savin-Williams, R. C. (1993). Personal reflections on coming out, prejudice, and homophobia in the academic workplace. In L. Diamant (ed.), *Homosexual issues in the workplace* (pp. 225-241). New York: Taylor & Francis.

Schneider, B. (1986). Coming out at work: Bridging the private/public gap. *Work and Occupations, 13,* 463-487.

Sears, J. T. (1992). Educators, homosexuality, and homosexual students: Are personal feelings related to professional beliefs? In K. Harbeck (Ed.), *Coming out of the classroom closet* (pp. 29-79). Binghamton, NY: Harrington Park Press.

Shevock, J. R., Hicks, T. L., Campbell, H., Sandbrook, D. L., Garcia, P., & Rodieck, R. R. (1992). *Sexual orientation: An issue of workplace diversity.* A Report by the Ad-Hoc Committee of the Regional Civil Rights Committee prepared for the Regional Forester, Pacific Southwest Region, USDA-Forest Service.

Smith, P. C., Kendall, L. M., & Hulin, C. L. (1969). *The measurement of satisfaction in work and retirement*. Chicago: Rand McNally.

Spielman, S., & Winfeld, L. (this volume). Domestic partner benefits: A bottom line discussion. *Journal of Gay & Lesbian Social Services*.

Sussal, C. M. (1994). Empowering gays and lesbians in the workplace. *Journal of Gay & Lesbian Social Services, 1*, 89-103.

Time/CNN Poll, *Time*, June 27, 1994 (p. 58).

Whitam, F. J., & Dizon, M. J. (1979). Occupational choice and sexual orientation in cross-cultural perspective. *International Review of Modern Sociology, 9*, 137-149.

Whitam, F. J., & Mathy, R. (1986). *Male homosexuality in four societies*. New York: Praeger.

Williamson, A. D. (1993). Is this the right time to come out? *Harvard Business Review*, July-August, 18-27.

Wolfson, E. (1994). *Out on the job, out of a job: A lawyers overview of the employment rights of lesbians and gay men*. New York: Lambda Legal Defense and Education Fund.

Woods, J. (with J. Lucas). (1993). *The corporate closet*. New York: The Free Press.

Work in America: Report of a special task force to the Secretary of Health, Education, and Welfare. (1973). Cambridge, MA: MIT Press.

Multicultural Existence in the Workplace: Including How I Thrive as a Latina Lesbian Feminist

Gina Scuteri Rosabal

SUMMARY. This essay will examine some of the issues that queer workers must deal with, with particular attention to the dynamics of multiple undervalued identities of individuals in the workplace. The interplay of racism, sexism and homophobia is explored focusing on three key areas: special challenges in the workplace; advancement concerns; and safety issues and survival strategies. It also examines the impact of internalized homophobia and horizontal hostility in each of these areas. While grounded in my personal standpoints, as a Latina and Lesbian in academia, the issues raised have broader applications for diverse individuals across a variety of occupational settings. *[Article copies available from The Haworth Document Delivery Service: 1-800-342-9678.]*

The dynamics of sex, race, and sexual orientation in the workplace are increasingly being identified and explored by both social service

---

Gina Scuteri Rosabal, PhD, is Assistant Professor of Women's Studies at Mankato State University.

The author acknowledges with great appreciation the helpful comments of Genet Pierce and Liz Frawley.

Address correspondence to Department of Women's Studies, Box 64, Mankato State University, Mankato, MN 56002-8400.

[Haworth co-indexing entry note]: "Multicultural Existence in the Workplace: Including How I Thrive as a Latina Lesbian Feminist." Rosabal, Gina Scuteri. Co-published simultaneously in *Journal of Gay & Lesbian Social Services* (The Haworth Press, Inc.) Vol. 4, No. 4, 1996, pp. 17-28; and: *Sexual Identity on the Job: Issues and Services* (ed: Alan L. Ellis, and Ellen D. B. Riggle) The Haworth Press, Inc., 1996, pp. 17-28; and: *Sexual Identity on the Job: Issues and Services* (ed: Alan L. Ellis, and Ellen D. B. Riggle) Harrington Park Press, an imprint of The Haworth Press, Inc., 1996, pp. 17-28. Single or multiple copies of this article are available from The Haworth Document Delivery Service [1-800-342-9678, 9:00 a.m. - 5:00 p.m. (EST)].

© 1996 by The Haworth Press, Inc. All rights reserved.

organizations and academics. Unfortunately, each of these components is usually explored in isolation, as though individuals were unidimensional rather than multidimensional. [The works of several women of color (some of whom are also queer) provide notable exceptions; particularly Anzaldua (1987, 1990), Collins (1991), hooks (1981, 1984, 1989, 1990), Lorde (1984), Lugones & Spelman (1983), and Moraga (1981).]

Strategies for change allege that if racism is eliminated, sexism will collapse; or that if class oppression is eliminated, all other oppressions will follow. Individuals are asked to fragment themselves; to choose sides rather than "divide" the movement or "dilute" the issue.[1] However, as multidimensional individuals, it is vital that we understand the dynamics of multiple identities in a society which justifies its division of power based on characteristics such as race, class, gender, and sexual orientation. In order for the social service professional to be effective, an understanding of these intersections is crucial.

Using a multidimensional approach reminds us of our specific standpoints[2] within our general discussions. For example, while many of the issues facing lesbians are shared with our gay brothers and bisexual and transgender siblings, others are unique to lesbians, and while some aspects of racism are shared across races, others are specific to one group. Throughout this essay, my discussions of sexism, racism and homophobia are informed by broader theoretical knowledge, but *grounded* in my personal standpoints as Latina and as Lesbian. Likewise, many of the workplace issues that we confront are similar across a wide range of occupational settings, enabling me to discuss the workplace on a broader scope, although I will draw on my personal experience within academia for specific examples. Social service providers in the workplace need to become familiar with all three of these dimensions of bias, as well as their interplay, and also to familiarize themselves with the politics of word choices in discussing these issues.

There is widespread disagreement about the terminology used by and about the queer community. I have chosen to use the term "queer" for a variety of reasons; key among these are reclamation, inclusion, and brevity. Much as Lesbians have reclaimed the term "dyke," gay men have reclaimed the term "faerie," and the queer communities have reclaimed the pink and the black triangles, we are also reclaiming the term "queer." (For a detailed discussion of reclamation in the queer community, see Grahn, 1984.) It is a deliberate political choice, empowering our communities by simultaneously naming ourselves (rather than accepting externally determined terminology) and by removing the power that homophobic individuals wielded by using that term against us. Inclusion is a second reason behind this choice. Bisexual and transgender people continue to struggle against invisibility in both the heterosexual environments and in the queer communities. Many of the support services and most of the written resources are labeled "Lesbian and Gay." The term "queer" is a more inclusive term, although we each have a responsibility to ensure that that inclusion is reflected in content and practice as well; and in instances where inclusion is not a reality, different terminology should be used. Finally, the term queer provides a refreshing brevity as alternative to repeatedly stating "Lesbian, Gay, Bisexual and Transgender."

A final introductory note–too often our recent visibility has taken the form of "victimization identity"; focusing almost exclusively on oppression. While there is a need to identify, understand, and eliminate areas of oppression, our queer identity (and identity of color, gender, etc.) is *also* the source of much joy, creativity, growth, and strength. Our struggles against interlocking systems of oppression, our personal, political, and social victories, and our survival are equally important aspects of our identity. Just as we grow from refusing to fragment ourselves into single components of our identity, we gain strength and celebration from exploring and presenting a balanced picture of who we are. It is vital for social service workers to understand not only the oppression but also the benefits and positive aspects to queer identity. Only through this balanced understanding can helping professionals assist workers in achieving their full potential.

SPECIAL CHALLENGES IN THE WORKPLACE

All queer workers, unless employed in queer organizations, must face the questions of if, when, and to whom to come out on the job. If in addition to being queer, race and gender dynamics come into play, these questions take on new dimensions. For example, if you are the only woman or the only person of color at your workplace, coming out carries a lot more risk (and you might also ask yourself why other women or people of color have not been hired at your workplace). In many cases, as a "representative"[3] of your race and/or gender, there may be a higher level of scrutiny of your job performance (and probably your personal life as well). Moreover, you may be dealing with sexism and/or racism from your co-workers, employees, or supervisors. Deciding whether to risk dealing with homophobia as well can be unnerving. Another factor in the decision process is class status, which plays a key role in the extent to which you are able to risk losing your job by choosing to come out.

The decision can be further complicated if there *are* a few other women and/or people of color with whom you work, and you are not out to them. In that instance, you risk losing the small pockets of support that you have found in an otherwise hostile or unfriendly environment. The phenomenon known as "horizontal hostility" plays itself out when persons who are being oppressed turn their anger at those who have equal or less power/status. Since they are unable to risk retaliation from those with higher power/status, they will often lash out at co-workers, employees, spouses, or children. These oppressed workers/individuals may also discover that they are "rewarded" by co-workers and supervisors if they collaborate in the discrimination of an "other" (the queer worker, female worker, or worker of color) or are punished for siding with that "other" worker against discrimination. Consequently, the queer worker must weigh several dynamics and risk factors in determining whether to come out.

There is debate within queer communities about whether it is preferable to let heterosexuals "get to know you as a person" first, and then come out, or to *be* out among others as you meet them. This debate carries over into the "timing questions" of coming out at the workplace: is it preferable to be "out" while interviewing for jobs (even if that means risking the loss of potential jobs), or to wait until one has been hired and establishes herself or himself as a "good" worker and colleague? Although each individual must ulti- mately make her or his own choice on this matter, there is ample documentation to support the positive correlation between being out and better mental health.[4] Being closeted at work takes an enormous amount of energy and creates tremendous anxiety. It also creates isolation. Living in constant fear of being "found out," constantly watching one's pronouns, being evasive about one's home life and leisure activities, attending work-related social functions with a phony escort or alone—these are but a few examples of the costs of being closeted at work. [For a thorough and insightful discussion of these issues, see McNaught, 1993.]

When I went on the job market four years ago, I made a deliberate choice to identify myself both as Lesbian and as Latina, and to seek out information about the environment that I could expect as a member of both groups, as well as being a woman. I made a list of specific questions to ask and specific warning signs to look out for in determining whether or not a potential job was a good match. Both the tone and the content of these questions are important. For example, instead of asking "*do* you have any specific strategies in place for the recruitment and retention of Latina and/or Lesbian faculty, staff and students?" I would ask "*what* specific strategies do you have . . . ?" Other important questions include whether sexual orientation is a specifically protected category in their non-discrimination policy; which of your benefits extend to a same-sex partner; what kind of diversity (both in terms of people and curriculum) already exists and at what levels; whether things like Latino food and music are readily available in the community; etc. Negative answers to these questions, discomfort discussing these issues, or evasive responses are strong warning signs to search elsewhere.

I felt strongly that if I were to be denied a job due to lesbophobia or racism, then that work environment would not be one in which I could be myself, let alone thrive. The word "choice" in this statement is deliberate. While some may feel that it is a matter of semantics, I am convinced that it is crucial to distinguish between being denied a job due to homophobia and being denied the job because one is queer. The former identifies the issue as external to the queer individual, and places the burden of responsibility with the bigoted potential employer. The latter unfairly blames the victim and contributes to internalized homophobia. The former indicates an institutional problem; the latter, a personal character flaw. The same argument can be made for racism and sexism. These distinctions also point to the importance of adding "sexual orientation" to workplace non-discrimination policies, thereby providing the worker with legal protection, defining discrimination as unacceptable behavior from co-workers or supervisors, and placing the burden on the employer rather than the worker.

I have not once regretted the decision to be out while searching for a job. I am comfortably out in my classrooms, in my writing, and in all other facets of my work environment. This article is a good example. If I were closeted at work, my publications would be greatly censored, excluding both queer issues and queer publications. However, "finding community" at work becomes much more complicated with multiple facets to one's identity. I still struggle with racism within the queer community and feminist community, and with sexism and homophobia within the Latino/Chicano community.

ADVANCEMENT CONCERNS

There are three key interrelated areas affecting advancement for workers juggling multiple identities: assimilation, "legitimacy," and multiple time demands. Assimilation can take a number of forms. In terms of a queer identity, it entails assimilating into a heterosexist work environment. If a heterosexual co-worker has a photo of her or his partner on the desk, or discusses family activities, then that co-worker is "sharing." If the queer worker does the same, she or he is "flaunting" or "pushing their sexual identities down the throats" of other workers. If the queer worker raises questions about the disparity in benefits available to partners of queer workers and heterosexual workers, the queer worker is often labeled a "troublemaker." What the heterosexual worker has is "status quo"; what the queer worker wants is "rocking the boat." "Rocking the boat" seldom gets one promoted.

Similar issues arise for a female worker in a predominately male-defined workplace. Different–and often conflicting–expectations are placed upon the female worker. If she acts "like a woman," she is perceived as less professional and less competent. If she acts "like a man," she becomes a "dragon-lady." Women are expected to take greater care with their physical appearance and dress–often held to dress code expectations that have no parallel among their male colleagues. The racial "norm" in the workplace is also frequently defined as white. In order to "fit in," workers of color are expected to speak, dress, and act "like white people." Having a strong sense of identity *as* a woman or as a person of color can be very threatening to white or male co-workers or supervisors, who often perceive this strength as an "anti-male" and/or "anti-white" attitude.

Mentors often play a significant role in guiding junior workers through the processes that lead to promotions. For the queer and/or female and/or of color worker[5] such a person may be hard to find. If such a person is available, she or he is often in a double-bind. If these workers take on the role of mentor, co-workers or supervisors may feel threatened by what they perceive as the formation of an "us vs. them" dynamic.[6] If they choose not to take on this role, they may be perceived by the person seeking mentorship as being assimilated or tokenized; as having a lot of internalized oppression, or as being willing to sacrifice their "own kind" in exchange for not threatening the dominant group. Social service professionals can help to address this by making management more aware of the need for mentors with similar cultures and perspectives, as well as the benefits of mentorship to the worker, the mentor, and the entire organization.

Another issue that might arise is that racist and/or sexist and/or homophobic failures to promote the worker may be rationalized in terms of maintaining a harmonious workplace. This is based on the assumption that the other workers would be more comfortable with someone who "fits in" better. It is difficult to document discrimination of this sort, and workers may be more likely to leave their jobs in search of more equitable workplaces rather than to remain and attempt to seek redress. Again, there is a dire need for social service professionals to create the awareness needed to prevent these occurrences.

"Legitimacy" of one's workplace activities is also a form of assimilation, but one which merits individual discussion. As with the areas discussed above, the standard or norm of "legitimate" workplace activities is almost always defined by the groups which hold power. Let us examine academia as a working example. In order to achieve promotion and tenure, faculty members are expected to (among other things) publish a certain number of scholarly articles in well-respected journals in our fields of study. Within many disciplines, "serious" scholarly research is about males, about heterosexuals, and about white people. This is so firmly entrenched, that it is not even necessary to identify it as such. However, if the research is about women, about queers, about people of color, it is clearly labeled as such. Moreover, once labeled as such, it becomes trivialized as "special interest" and suspect as "political."

There exists a similar hierarchy within journals. Consequently, the pressure to publish "legitimate" articles in "respected" journals is great if one expects to be promoted within the university system. For a Lesbian of color, this might require the simultaneous alienation of three major self-identifying components. Likewise, for workers in other public or private sectors, attending a workshop on "business writing" may be seen as legitimate, while attending a workshop on "diversity in the workplace" may not. Social service providers need to work to make both types of training or assistance "legitimate," and to encourage that workshops on unlearning sexism, racism, homophobia, and other oppressive behavior be required of *all* workers.[7] (For an excellent blueprint for running an antihomophobia workshop, see Blumenfeld, 1992, pp. 275-302.)

The worker juggling multiple identities must also juggle multiple time demands, many of which are not "counted" towards promotion or tenure. These individuals are often expected to serve as mentors for every individual who shares one of their "characteristics." If the work environment is one in which many tasks are performed by committees, these workers are likely to be asked to serve on a very high number of committees, as a "representative" of their race, gender, or sexual orientation. They may be expected to keep current on news and scholarship directly affecting "their people," or be asked on a regular basis to speak to other groups about "their issues." This is, of course, *in addition to* their "regular" work. Helping professionals can help to ease this "extra burden" by regularly disseminating information about race, gender, and sexual orientation so that others are informed.

SAFETY ISSUES AND SURVIVAL STRATEGIES

The Hate Crimes Statistics Act, introduced in 1988 and signed into law in 1990, "required the Department of Justice to collect and publish annual statistics on crimes that manifest prejudice based on race, religion, sexual orientation, and ethnic origin" (Herek & Berrill, 1992). Feminists have also argued, with limited success, for the inclusion of gender as a category against which hate crimes are committed. Hate speech and other hate crimes may also occur at the workplace, and for the worker with multiple identities the risks are multiplied. As of 1992, "only two studies [had] examined racial and ethnic differences in rates of victimization. Both [had] found lesbians and gay men of color to be at increased risk for violent attack because of their sexual orientation" (Berrill, 1992). Although the studies did not specifically examine the workplace, this trend may apply across environments. Harassment remains a significant safety issue at the workplace. However, fear of reprisal, particularly if the perpetrator is a supervisor, may prove to be an obstacle to reporting the hate crime and prosecuting the perpetrator. This fear is greatly exacerbated if the worker is closeted.

If the worker with multiple identities chooses to file a grievance, she or he is likely to be asked to choose which form of discrimination to file the grievance under. This fragments the individual, obscures the interconnections between racism, sexism, and homophobia, and deprives the worker of relevant portions of substantiating documentation which may not be deemed "relevant" to the area of discrimination under which the grievance is filed. For example, if a woman of color who is being both sexually and racially harassed decides that she has a stronger case by filing under sexual harassment, she will not be able to provide evidence of racial harassment to substantiate her case. It is vital to begin to change institutional policies which require that recipients of multiple forms of harassment turn their multidimensional oppression into a unidimensional grievance.

There are, however, survival strategies for dealing with hate crimes in the workplace. An important first step for all workers, but especially those with multiple cultural identities, is to investigate their legal rights–from workplace policies to local, state, and federal laws. Awareness of your rights and options may deter perpetrators, particularly if they can expect disciplinary action, and it is likely to empower you by diminishing your own sense of helplessness or victimization.

In addition, the development of both personal and institutional support systems is *vital*. Personal support systems–both at and beyond the workplace–can serve to generate ideas about dealing with the situation, and help you to keep perspective of the accountability of the perpetrator (rather than internalizing the harassment and blaming yourself). Allies may serve as escorts if your physical safety is in question. Institutional support systems can diffuse an existing negative situation and prevent a potential one. For example, a commitment to providing increased anti-bias education and sensitivity training is likely to result in both attitudinal and behavioral changes at the workplace. Workshops on "unlearning" racism, sexism, and homophobia send a clear message that discrimination will not be tolerated; and they challenge the workers who hold these biases to explore and work through them.

Learning about and strengthening your own identities is a strategy that moves you *beyond* survival and enables you to thrive. Each of the identities discussed throughout this essay has been consistently undervalued in U.S. society. It is impossible to grow up in a sexist, racist, and homophobic society without learning and internalizing these messages. However, it is possible to *unlearn* them.

The first step is to seek out information and history that have been made invisible about queers/women/people of color. Seek out information written by members of these groups about their own experiences and history. Explore the aspects of your identity that give you strength and inform your leadership. Make connections with others in your group/s, and insist on being a "whole" person in each of these groups. Discuss sexism, racism, and homophobia openly with others in your group–not only in the abstract, but in terms of specific comments and actions. Share resources that you find with others. If you are an ally or a social service professional, make sure that you take responsibility for learning this information and for passing along these resources to others who need them.

NOTES

1. This has been a recurring charge levied at early suffragists by male abolitionists, at women activists in the New Left and the African American Civil Rights Movements, at Latina and Chicana activists in the Chicano Rights Movement, at Lesbians in the Gay Liberation Movement, and at women in numerous other movements.

2. I use the term "standpoint" in the epistemological sense: to indicate that knowledge is socially situated and socially constructed, and that the social division of power and status causes individuals in different social groups to have different sets of experiences and to develop particular vantage points and interpretive frameworks.

3. This is yet another area where social service professionals can make a difference. Employers and co-workers must be made aware that queer workers (or women workers or workers of color) are neither "test-cases" for determining whether others "like them" will "work out," nor spokespersons for their entire communities.

4. The most well-known developmental model of the "coming out" process identifies six stages, with a clear connection between self-acceptance and pride, and coming out (Cass, 1979). The highest three stages are "identity acceptance," "identity pride," and "identity synthesis," with the final stage requiring that "the person accepts her or his gay or lesbian orientation as one part of the person's identity" (Dworkin & Gutierrez 1992). Concealing a central part of that identity is inconsistent with achieving this level of synthesis. Also, thinking of one's identity as a shameful secret that others might discover exacerbates the internalization of homophobia.

5. Drawing attention to each of these characteristics individually, as well as in possible combinations, may seem cumbersome. Not doing so is a form of the assimilation described earlier.

6. The other extreme is that queer workers/workers of color/women workers are expected to take on the mentorship of all workers/students with similar characteristics.

7. If these workshops are voluntary, they are likely to "preach to the converted" rather than reaching those individuals most in need of the training. They may also pose difficult choices for closeted queer workers.

REFERENCES

Anzaldua, G. (1987). *Borderlands/La Frontera: The new mestiza.* San Francisco: Aunt Lute Press.

Anzaldua, G. (Ed.). (1990). *Making face/making soul/haciendo caras: Creative and critical perspectives by feminists of color.* San Francisco: Aunt Lute.

Blumenfeld, W. J. (1992). *Homophobia: How we all pay the price.* Boston: Beacon Press.

Cass, V. (1979). Homosexual identity formation: A theoretical model. *Journal of Homosexuality, 4,* 219-235.

Collins, P. H. (1991). *Black feminist thought: Knowledge, consciousness, and the politics of empowerment.* New York: Routledge.

Dworkin, S., & Gutierrez, F. (Eds.). (1992). *Counseling gay men and lesbians: Journey to the end of the rainbow.* Alexandria, VA: American Association for Counseling and Development.

Grahn, J. (1984). *Another mother tongue: Gay words, gay worlds.* Boston: Beacon Press.

Herek, G. M., & Berrill, K. T. (Eds.). (1992). *Hate crimes: Confronting violence against lesbians and gay men.* Newbury Park, CA: Sage Publications.

hooks, b. (1981). *Ain't I a woman: Black women and feminism.* Boston: South End Press.

hooks, b. (1984). *Feminist theory from margin to center.* Boston: South End Press.

hooks, b. (1989). *Talking back: Thinking feminist* thinking black.* Boston: South End Press.

hooks, b. (1990). *Yearning: Race, gender, and cultural politics.* Boston: South End Press.

Lorde, A. (1984). *Sister outsider.* New York: The Crossing Press.

Lugones, M., & Spelman, E. (1983). Have we got a theory for you! Feminist theory, cultural imperialism, and the demand for 'The woman's voice.' *Women's Studies International Forum, 6,* 573-581.

McNaught, B. (1993). *Gay issues in the workplace.* New York: St. Martin's Press.

Moraga, C., & Anzaldua, G. (1981). *This bridge called my back: Writings by radical women of color.* New York: Kitchen Table Press.

Employment and Sexual Orientation: Disclosure and Discrimination in the Workplace

M. V. Lee Badgett

SUMMARY. Economists, sociologists, and other social scientists have begun to study the influence of sexual orientation on individuals in the labor market, particularly with respect to employment discrimination. The conceptual framework developed in this paper connects lesbian, gay, and bisexual workers' disclosure of their sexual orientation to the economic and social characteristics of the workplace. Disclosure creates the potential for discrimination by employers and coworkers. The framework shows how sexual orientation operates independently and in interaction with other important characteristics such as race and gender. A review of existing research supports the hypothesis that discrimination against gay workers exists. Both workplace groups for gays and lesbians and those who

M. V. Lee Badgett, PhD, is Assistant Professor, School of Public Affairs, University of Maryland, College Park, MD 20742-1821.

Lisa Moore, Rhonda Williams, Katie King, Richard Cornwall, and Ellen Riggle provided helpful comments and conversations. I also received useful suggestions from participants at the University of Maryland Women's Studies Research Forum and from a panel at the 1992 American Economic Association Meeting, where I presented earlier versions of this paper. Also, I would like to thank Carol Ness of the *San Francisco Examiner*, Steve Teichner, Jeffrey Escoffier, *Out/Look* magazine, and the National Gay and Lesbian Task Force for providing me with unpublished data from their surveys.

[Haworth co-indexing entry note]: "Employment and Sexual Orientation: Disclosure and Discrimination in the Workplace." Badgett, M. V. Lee. Co-published simultaneously in *Journal of Gay & Lesbian Social Services* (The Haworth Press, Inc.) Vol. 4, No. 4, 1996, pp. 29-52; and: *Sexual Identity on the Job: Issues and Services* (ed: Alan L. Ellis, and Ellen D. B. Riggle) The Haworth Press, Inc., 1996, pp. 29-52; and: *Sexual Identity on the Job: Issues and Services* (ed: Alan L. Ellis, and Ellen D. B. Riggle) Harrington Park Press, an imprint of The Haworth Press, Inc., 1996, pp. 29-52. Single or multiple copies of this article are available from The Haworth Document Delivery Service [1-800-342-9678, 9:00 a.m. - 5:00 p.m. (EST)].

© 1996 by The Haworth Press, Inc. All rights reserved.   *29* work with gay and lesbian workers (such as supervisors, personnel managers, and counselors) need to understand the relationship between disclosure and discrimination in order to make workplaces supportive of lesbian, gay, and bisexual workers. *[Article copies available from The Haworth Document Delivery Service: 1-800-342-9678.]*

INTRODUCTION

For many years, social scientists have worked to understand how social forces influence individuals in the United States labor market. Economists and sociologists, in particular, have long studied labor market discrimination against women and people of color. In expanding our view to apply similar methods and questions to discrimination because of sexual orientation, however, we must proceed carefully to avoid the overgeneralization that the sources and effects of discrimination are identical for all oppressed groups. When we inquire into the existence of discrimination against lesbians, gay men, and bisexuals, we increase our understanding of forces that influence an individual's labor market position, forces which include race, gender, and class. This paper develops a conceptual framework that shows how a worker's sexual orientation may have independent effects within the workplace and interactive effects with other socially and economically relevant characteristics, mainly race and gender, as well as how the awareness of these effects is relevant to those who work with lesbian, gay, and bisexual individuals.

Extending the scope of labor market research to include the topic of sexual orientation has obvious academic appeal as more widespread interest in lesbian/gay/bisexual studies grows. But this expansion is more than an academic adventure into uncharted territory, as discrimination against gay and bisexual people has become the subject of intense policy and political debate, mainly focusing on whether discrimination against gay people truly exists. In the 1992 elections, opponents of lesbian and gay civil rights forced referenda that would have repealed local gay rights laws in Oregon, Colorado, Tampa, Florida, and Portland, Maine. (At the time of this writing, the Colorado gay rights law was reinstated by the courts.) These campaigns, which were successful statewide in Colorado and citywide in Tampa, shared the argument that such civil rights laws granted gay men and lesbians "special privileges" or "special rights," a claim which clearly challenges the notion that gays and lesbians face discrimination in the labor market. Furthermore, literature published in the Colorado campaign asked:

> Are homosexuals a "disadvantaged" minority? You decide! Records show that even now, not only are gays not economically disadvantaged, they're actually one of the most affluent groups in America! On July 18, 1991, the *Wall Street Journal* reported the results of a nation-wide marketing survey about gay income levels. The survey reported that gays' average income was more than $30,000 over that of the average Americans' [sic]. (Colorado for Family Values, 1992)

The basic argument, then, seems to be that lesbians and gay men do not encounter discrimination since they seemed to have achieved unusual economic success without civil rights protections. (The serious flaws in this argument, mainly statistically biased samples and incorrect comparisons, will be discussed further.)

In addition to the academic and policy needs for an understanding of discrimination and its relationship to disclosure, those professionals working with lesbian, gay, and bisexual workers also need to recognize the complex set of influences that shape those workers' work lives and decisions. As gay issues become more prominent in the workplace, supervisors, counselors, and personnel managers must consider new questions: Should we encourage gay workers to come out, i.e., to disclose their sexual orientation within the workplace? Do our employment practices discriminate against gay workers in any way, and is discrimination illegal? How does dealing with sexual orientation fit in with other diversity issues? In seeking answers to these and other questions, human resources professionals must grapple with many of the same conceptual issues as social scientists.

In the next section, this paper offers an overview of the legal situation faced by lesbian, gay, and bisexual workers and shows that most of them have little legal protection against discrimination. Then a conceptual framework of the labor market role of sexual orientation is developed, which will help structure future empirical research and guide helping professionals. The framework connects gay workers' disclosure of their sexual orientation to workplace characteristics, including the workplace social climate and economic incentives, creating the potential for discrimination by employers and coworkers. This framework also reveals points of divergence in the workplace effects of sexual orientation for different race and gender groups. The last section examines existing evidence of discrimination and suggests several other research strategies.

CURRENT LEGAL SITUATION

The legal position of lesbian, gay, or bisexual workers differs between public and private employees. Gay and bisexual people have no explicit protection from employment discrimination at the federal level in the private sector. Eight states have civil rights laws that prohibit discrimination by private employers on the basis of sexual orientation: California, Connecticut, Hawaii, Massachusetts, Minnesota, New Jersey, Vermont, Wisconsin, and the District of Columbia. Many city and/or county laws also provide such legal protection. Estimates vary as to the number of private employers who have a nondiscrimination policy toward lesbians and gay men, but many large companies do have such policies (Martinez, 1993).

When not bound by a collective bargaining agreement or by civil rights laws, employers have traditionally been able to hire and fire employees at will. This employment-at-will doctrine has recently come under attack in a variety of contexts as courts increasingly find that implicit contractual limitations allow employers to fire employees only for cause (Editors of *Harvard Law Review*, 1991). This notion of an implied contract has been used with mixed results against employers who have fired employees because of their sexual orientation (Editors of *Harvard Law Review*, 1991). In a recent case, a California state judge found that Shell Oil wrongfully discharged an employee because of his homosexuality rather than for job performance, the criterion that Shell claimed guided all dismissal decisions (Shao, 1991). But this protection, like that afforded by union contracts, only protects those who are already employed.

Other laws limiting private employers' actions, particularly Title VII of the Civil Rights Act of 1964, have provided little protection against anti-gay discrimination.[1] The effect of existing local anti-discrimination ordinances in overturning discriminatory acts against lesbians and gay men is still unclear. Such ordinances often face rescission (as evidenced by the referenda noted earlier) and "may be unenforceable when they conflict with federal interests or constitutional rights" (Editors of *Harvard Law Review*, 1991).

Public employers operate under additional constraints not faced by private employers. Employees of 18 states are protected from discrimination by executive orders or state law (*Ten Percent*, 1993). Perhaps more importantly, the government's ability to hire and fire employees is limited by certain constitutional requirements. For federal employees, the Fifth and Fourteenth Amendments guarantee due process and equal protection under the law, respectively. Until recently, these constitutional principles have provided little employment protection for lesbian and gay public employees. Lower tier due process or equal protection review of a government action based on an employee's sexual orientation would require the government to show a "rational relationship between that person's sexual orientation and the efficiency of governmental operations" (Editors of *Harvard Law Review*, 1991). Courts have accepted numerous unsubstantiated rationales in upholding discriminatory actions against military personnel and against those seeking security clearances, but the rational relationship requirement provides some limited protection for civil servants (Editors of *Harvard Law Review*, 1991).

Two lower courts have considered sexual orientation as a "suspect" or "quasi-suspect" classification that requires what is known as "heightened equal protection scrutiny." This level of judicial scrutiny requires the government to demonstrate that the classification of people by their sexual orientation serves an "important" interest (if quasi-suspect) or a "compelling" government goal (if suspect) and bears a "substantial" relationship (quasi-suspect) or is "precisely tailored" (suspect) to the issue at hand (Editors of *Harvard Law Review*, 1991). The application of heightened scrutiny has not been upheld on appeal, but it has resulted in one case forcing the military to reinstate an openly gay soldier (Watkins v. U.S. Army) (ACLU, 1991). The Supreme Court has yet to rule on whether sexual orientation is either a suspect classification, as is race, or quasi-suspect, as is sex (Editors of *Harvard Law Review,* 1991).

As this section demonstrates, when most lesbian, gay, or bisexual people arrive at their workplaces, they are vulnerable to the kind of discrimination from which heterosexual women and heterosexual people of color are legally protected. And although thirty years of federal antidiscrimination policies have not completely eliminated sex and race discrimination (see, for example, Turner, Fix, & Struyk, 1991), those forms of discrimination can be fought through administrative and judicial processes. Professionals who work with gay workers and want to integrate gay workers more fully into their workplaces must recognize this real vulnerability that makes gay workers' situation very different from other protected categories, such as race, gender, and disability status.

CONCEPTUAL FRAMEWORK

Studying labor market discrimination means drawing causal links between an individual's sexual orientation and her/his labor market outcomes–hiring, promotion, wages, employment status, etc. This requires some understanding of the role of sexuality in the economy, an understanding that economists, in particular, are only beginning to develop (see Badgett & Williams, 1992; Posner, 1992; Matthaei, 1993). The approach here is to consider only one dimension of sexuality: the fact that some individuals' sexual partners are of the same gender. This framework takes as given the existence of homophobia (the fear of homosexuals and homosexuality) and heterosexism (the belief that heterosexuality is superior and should be an enforceable social norm) but acknowledges that these social attitudes vary in existence and intensity across individuals over time.[2] In this paper, the main question considers how homophobic or heterosexist attitudes in the workplace affect a lesbian, gay, or bisexual worker.

Identity and Behavior. While the ways that race and gender operate within the economy are complex, at least those who study these factors (and human resources professionals working with women and people of color) have the empirical advantage of studying an observable attribute.[3] Because someone's sexuality is not easily observed or inferred, the option of hiding it in some or all social contexts is often chosen by lesbian, gay, or bisexual people to avoid the potential for social ostracism, physical violence, or other sanctions imposed by an unaccepting society. To further complicate the issue of observability, the development of a lesbian, gay, or bisexual identity is a process that can occur at any stage of life and at different rates (Garnets & Kimmel, 1991). This hiddenness, whether from oneself or from others, makes standard research techniques (such as random sampling) extremely difficult and has impeded social scientific progress on issues of sexuality.

But hiding one's sexuality may also dampen the extent of social or economic sanctions faced by an individual, including employment discrimination. In this framework, the connection between sexuality and labor market outcomes hinges crucially on the issue of *disclosure* of lesbian, gay, or bisexual behavior and/or identity. And since hiding is associated with avoidance of sanctions, disclosure is likely to be at least partly determined by workplace factors.

Before further developing the relationship between disclosure and the workplace, at least some discussion of the thorny issue of the relationship between behavior (sexual practices) and identity (considering oneself lesbian, gay, or bisexual) is in order.[4] The assumption in this framework is that both behavior and identity are sufficient to trigger sanctions. For instance, the *act* of sodomy is still prohibited in almost half of the states (Editors of *Harvard Law Review*, 9), as is the solicitation of "noncommercial, consensual same-sex sexual activity" in many places (Editors of *Harvard Law Review*, 1991). Those laws have sometimes been explicitly used to justify employment discrimination against gay people (Rubenstein, 1993). And recent political efforts notwithstanding, homosexual acts are still grounds for discharge from the military (Editors of *Harvard Law Review*, 1991).

Within the workplace, however, having a gay identity may be more problematic than behavior. Identity suggests the potential for joining other lesbian or gay employees in collective action that challenges existing employment practices and the workplace social environment. For instance, gay employees have formed groups that have pressured employers to provide benefits for domestic partners, presenting a challenge to compensation plans built upon the heterosexual bias of the legal institution of marriage (see Building Community at PG&E, 1992). Fears of similar action may intensify homophobic attitudes of employers and coworkers toward individual gay-identified workers.

Using sexual orientation broadly also avoids the potential for bias that arises from different cultural relationships between behavior and identity. For example, Alonso and Koreck (1989) point out that in some Mexican and Central American cultures, men who have sex with other men do not necessarily identify themselves as either homosexual or bisexual. Only some of those men, those playing the passive roles, are stigmatized for their sexual practices within their own culture.

Disclosure. While the question of disclosure relates both to behavior and to identity, the issue of voluntary disclosure may relate more to identity, given the general political strategy for the lesbian and gay liberation movement since the 1970s of "coming out." For simplicity, most of the discussion will consider the voluntary disclosure of one's lesbian, gay, or bisexual identity.[5] The framework first posits a relationship between the work environment and disclosure and then shows how disclosure may affect an individual's labor market position. Table 1 summarizes five categories of factors in a rough linear approximation of the causal links between sexuality and labor market effects. The relationship among the elements of

TABLE 1. Elements of Theoretical Framework

Sexuality	Workplace	Disclosure	To Whom	Labor Mkt. Effects
Behavior	Stress on passing	Voluntary	Coworkers	None
		Involuntary	Boss	None
Identity	Sociability			Discrimination: Job loss
	Income			No promotion Harassment
		None/passing		Lower productivity, absenteeism

the categories is complicated, of course, and the individual elements will be woven together in the following discussion.

The Work Environment and Disclosure. Work environments vary along several social dimensions related to sexual orientation. Escoffier (1975) categorizes occupational and job characteristics based on "the stress laid on passing and individual success at passing," where "passing" refers to concealing one's sexual orientation: (1) "Conservative" occupations that allow no deviations from the heterosexual norm, e.g., military jobs, elementary school teaching, and certain corporate occupations; (2) "liberal" occupations that are more likely to be tolerant, in which individual productivity is easier to measure; and (3) "ghetto" occupations "that are publicly labeled as predominantly open to gay people or . . . employ many gay people." Escoffier suggests that the occupational choices of a lesbian or gay man will depend on the value of passing to that person. In other words, Escoffier focuses on the way that an individual's preferences regarding disclosure determine his or her work environment.

Survey data provide some support for Escoffier's hypothesis. In a national survey conducted by Steve Teichner for the *San Francisco Examiner*, 15% of the men and 19% of the women said that their sexual orientation played a major role in selecting their job or profession. (The unpublished data from this survey were provided to the author for independent analysis). The small proportions may not be surprising considering that many people develop a lesbian, gay, or bisexual identity after they have already begun a job or career. And Escoffier notes that those who do come out at a younger age have a hard time getting useful input on the differences in work environments at the time they are making education and training decisions.

Schneider (1986) proposed a model to explain the other direction of influence: how the work environment influences a lesbian's propensity to disclose her lesbianism to coworkers. In Schneider's model, workplaces vary according to whether they create "a context conducive to intimacy and self-disclosure." She tested the model using nonrandom survey data from 228 lesbians and allowed sociability and disclosure to be jointly determined in her statistical method. The results revealed that a lesbian's degree of disclosure increased in human service occupations and with a higher percentage of women in the department or workplace. Working with children, having a higher income, and experiencing a previous job loss from disclosure all decreased the degree of disclosure.

Sociability may also be an important factor *within* groups of lesbian, gay, and bisexual workers in the same workplace. Some workplace groups of gay employees have formalized (see Building Community at PG&E, 1992; Woods, 1993), and even informal groups that may provide enough social and political support for gay employees to come out. As noted earlier, these groups often work for nondiscrimination policies in employment and benefits, and disclosure may be an important part of the intra-company lobbying process.

Income and Disclosure. Putting the two models together provides a more complex understanding of the relationship between a person's management of disclosure and her/his work environment. To add further complexity, economic aspects of the workplace are also likely to be related to disclosure. Schneider's data show a negative relationship between income and disclosure: higher income lesbians disclose less (Schneider, 1986). The more recent Teichner/ *San Francisco Examiner* survey data suggest that this relationship may not be so clear-cut and may have even changed. Table 2 shows an inverted V relationship: disclosure increases with income to a point (the 50,000-60,000 range in the national sample and the 30,000-40,000 range in the Bay Area sample) and then declines at higher income levels.

TABLE 2. Relationship Between Income and Disclosure to Coworkers

| | % out to coworkers | |
Annual Income	National	Bay Area
Less than 10,000	42	48
10,000-20,000	48	53
20,000-30,000	51	63
30,000-40,000	58	70
40,000-50,000	64	62
50,000-60,000	78	52
60,000-70,000	40	49
over 70,000	64	57

Source: Unpublished cross-tabulations from the 1989 Teichner/*San Francisco Examiner* survey.

This relationship might be a result of the lack of controls for age or workplace sociability, but the data in Table 2 are provocative. Income could certainly have conflicting influences on disclosure. On one hand, individuals with higher incomes have more to lose if disclosure results in job loss, motivating a negative relationship between income and disclosure (Schneider, 1986). On the other hand, higher incomes may reflect more authority and power in the workplace and, therefore, a greater ability to overcome or neutralize negative reactions to disclosure. Higher income might then be related to a lower risk of total loss and thus to greater disclosure. Given the figures in Table 2, both effects may be at work, with middle-range income acting as a switching point.

Two other economic models generalize the relationship between income and workplace disclosure. If an individual uses a simple cost-benefit approach to make disclosure decisions, she or he will compare the likely benefits, such as enhanced self-esteem or a more accepting and supportive workplace (Woods, 1993), to the possible cost of coming out, such as lost income from fewer promotions or job loss. Although the value of these benefits may vary somewhat from person to person, the possible costs will probably vary more since income varies greatly among individuals. A person earning a high income may find that the relative cost of coming out is high compared to the benefits, but a low income person may find the relative cost of coming out to be lower compared to the benefits (which may be roughly the same as for a high income worker). Thus, according to this model, gay people earning higher incomes will disclose less than lower income people.

An investment model of disclosure (a more elaborate cost-benefit approach) provides an approach that more explicitly accounts for risk and for future benefits: Given the risk of economic harm, lesbians and gay men may trade-off career advancement or security for a future return when making their disclosure decisions (Woods, 1993). Risk depends on the social nature of the workplace and on the lesbian or gay worker's ability to manage any negative reactions. Workers assess risk over time and may do so at the level of the overall workplace as well as the level of the individual co-worker or boss. The future return may again be thought of as psychological or as political. Modelling disclosure as an investment good, then, implies that, all else equal, more may be "purchased" by individuals with higher incomes who "pay" for coming out in terms of income placed at risk.

Describing the disclosure decision process in these ways is intended not to completely represent the process but to highlight the potential importance of income. The income effect will be important in constructing and interpreting future empirical work on the effects of sexual orientation on income (discussed in the next section), as well as for interpreting how representative members of gay workplace groups are of an employer's entire group of gay workers. The income effect will also influence the distribution of the benefits of any policy changes that require disclosure, such as declaration of domestic partnerships to get employment benefits.

Disclosure and Discrimination. Two important additional points must be made regarding disclosure. First, involuntary disclosure of a gay employee's sexual orientation, sometimes known as "outing," can occur in many ways. Inferences of identity or behavior can be made from military and police records, marital status, neighborhood of residence, silences in conversations, etc. Furthermore, voluntary disclosures to coworkers increase the likelihood of either accidental or deliberate involuntary disclosure to others. The case of Jeffrey Collins, the Shell Oil employee mentioned earlier, illustrates the damaging effects of a series of involuntary disclosures. Collins accidentally left a copy of "house rules" for a gay sex party at the computer printer. Another employee found the copy and circulated it, resulting in Collins being fired. Shell later notified headhunters of the reason for Collins's dismissal, reducing his chances for obtaining a new job (Shao, 1991).

The second additional point is that a choice not to disclose involves ambiguous economic effects. Escoffier points out that passing may require avoidance of social interactions that contribute to advancement and job satisfaction for other workers (also, see Woods, 1993). This social isolation could lead to higher absenteeism and job turnover, and the energy devoted to passing might reduce both productivity and incomes. But this costly behavior does not justify discrimination. The behavior is not an intrinsic characteristic of the worker but a result of the work environment and could be thought of as a form of *indirect* discrimination. Alternatively, passing could improve gay workers' productivity if, as Mohr (1988) argues, gay workers ". . . respond to the threat of employment discrimination by becoming workaholics."

Disclosure, whether voluntary or involuntary, can result in sanctions by coworkers, supervisors, or employers. Homophobic or heterosexist reactions by coworkers might reduce the gay worker's income, productivity, and/or advancement. Homophobic supervisors can harass, fire, or refuse to promote lesbian, gay, or bisexual employees. These negative reactions, while at least partly the result of individual attitudes toward gay people, are also likely to be influenced by the work environment. And negative reactions are certain to feedback into a lesbian or gay worker's future disclosure decisions (as Schneider found), many of which are made knowing that legal recourse against discrimination does not exist. Ultimately, the overall extent of economic sanctions is an empirical question, as discussed below.

Race and Gender. One advantage of simplifying the disclosure process in this framework is that potential differences in disclosure between race and gender groups are immediately expected. Lesbians of color, white lesbians, and gay men of color must deal with the damaging effects of racism and sexism in the workplace. Would disclosing their sexual orientation add significantly or only slightly to the disadvantage that they may already face? Would disclosure of their sexual orientation push them over some threshold of the number of acceptable differences? Table 3 presents results from questions about workplace disclosure in two surveys. In both surveys, women indicate less workplace disclosure than men. The racial differences are less stark, with black respondents indicating different disclosure levels from white and Hispanic workers, but this is not consistent between the Bay Area survey and the national survey. Understanding the reason for these differences is not a simple project, but all three aspects of the relationship between disclosure and the workplace described in this section suggest differences in disclosure by race and gender.

The ability of an individual's preferences for disclosure to determine his or her occupation, the first aspect of the work-disclosure relationship, is likely to vary by race and gender. The degree of occupational choice available to an individual has varied signifi-

TABLE 3. Workplace Disclosure by Gender and Race

Out/Look, 1988: "Are you 'out' at your workplace?":

	Men	Women
to no one	8.0	17.2
to anyone	16.4	10.5
to more than two people	18.3	26.0
to the majority of your coworkers	23.0	24.3
to everyone you work with	34.3	22.0
Number of respondents:	213	296

Teichner/San Francisco Examiner: "Have you told your co-workers about your sexual orientation?"
National percentages (400 respondents):

	Men	Women	White	Black	Hispanic
Yes	62	33	57	40	62
No	36	64	42	60	38
Don't Know	2	3	2	--	--

Bay Area percentages (400 respondents):

	Men	Women	White	Black	Hispanic
Yes	62	53	61	89	69
No	38	47	39	11	31
Don't Know	--	--	--	--	--

Sources: unpublished data from both surveys.

cantly in the United States, with race and sex discrimination constraining the choices of women and people of color (see King, 1992, for an extensive and up-to-date discussion of occupational segregation by race and gender). Lesbian, gay, and bisexual people of color and white lesbians will thus have more limited occupational options than gay white men for reasons entirely separable from sexual orientation. To the extent that workplace sociability, the second part of the framework, varies by occupation, differences in the occupational distributions of race and gender groups will also lead to differences in the level of disclosure by race and gender.

Within occupations and particular jobs, lesbian and bisexual women may find that their gender is more of a disadvantage than their sexual orientation (Hall, 1989). Most economic studies show that married men's incomes are higher than unmarried men's, but married women's incomes are typically *lower* than unmarried women's incomes (e.g., Carlson & Swartz, 1988). This suggests that lesbians might actually benefit from the fact that they are (presumably) less likely to marry (i.e., to marry a man). Lesbians disclosing their sexual orientation could conceivably benefit by removing employers' fears or prejudices about their likelihood of marrying and quitting to raise a family (at least until same-sex relationships are allowed the same social and legal status as heterosexual marriages, in which case a lesbian "married" to another woman might be equally suspect in an employer's eyes). While seeing this marriage effect as a lesbian "advantage" may seem far-fetched, it at least suggests that relative to heterosexual women, disclosure as a lesbian might not make her as vulnerable as a gay man is relative to heterosexual men.

The greater overall economic vulnerability of lesbians as women would certainly affect lesbians' disclosure decisions. This vulnerability is found within the third aspect of the framework concerning the effect of income on disclosure. Persistent inequality in income by race and sex has been well-documented (see Blau & Beller, 1992, for a recent study) and thus might lead to differences in disclosure by both race and gender. This race-gender wedge occurs both *between* job categories (since white men tend to have higher paying jobs) and *within* job categories (see Bergmann, 1989, for evidence of gender pay differentials within detailed occupational categories).

The influence of income and occupation also suggests important class differences in disclosure. Even sociability within workplace groups of lesbian, gay, and bisexual workers could have important class implications if these organizations are founded by and composed of mainly managerial, professional, and technical employees.

Overall, then, while similar forces may nudge all lesbian, gay, and bisexual workers in the same directions in terms of disclosure, the differences in economic and workplace contexts that gay workers find themselves in because of their race and gender may lead to very different disclosure patterns. And differences in the social treatment of workers within workplaces because of racism and sexism may also influence disclosure of sexual orientation, although the effects of the interaction of these factors are as yet unclear. Supervisors, personnel managers, and counselors should recognize that sexual orientation must be considered alongside race and gender when working with white lesbians or gay men and lesbians of color.

IMPLICATIONS FOR RESEARCHERS
AND WORKPLACE PROFESSIONALS

Starting with a complex conceptual framework encourages comprehensive research strategies while leaving room for more partial and incremental approaches. Important and useful research on employment discrimination against lesbian and gay (and sometimes bisexual) people has been conducted that corroborates many of the assumptions embedded in the framework presented previously. The usefulness of these partial approaches for understanding the complexities discussed in this paper is limited by methodological problems common to much research on sexual orientation, however.

Perhaps the best documented assumption used in the framework is the existence of homophobic and heterosexist attitudes. Herek (1991) reviews public opinion survey data which shows persistent and widespread disapproval of homosexual behavior, but, in contrast, growing acceptance of the idea that gay people should have equal job opportunities. A survey of 191 Alaskan employers revealed that employers also have homophobic attitudes: 18% of those surveyed would fire, 27% would not hire, and 26% would not promote gay employees (Brause, 1989).

Court cases and surveys of self-identified lesbians and gay men demonstrate that attitudes may translate into actual discrimination. Table 4 summarizes selected surveys of self-identified lesbians and gay men who were asked about employment discrimination.[6] The proportion of lesbians or gay men who believe that they faced some form of employment discrimination (in hiring, promotion, or firing) during their working lives ranges from 13% to 62%. Unfortunately, these findings come from non-random samples,[7] making broader inferences impossible, and even a random sample might not reveal the true incidence of discrimination: actual discrimination may not be interpreted as such; perceived discrimination may be based on employers' legitimate non-discriminatory motives; and more discrimination might occur with wider knowledge of individuals' sexual orientation.

TABLE 4. Summary of Surveys of Employment Discrimination

Survey	Location	Year	Lifetime rate of Discrimination (%)			
Philadelphia	Philadelphia	1987	25	(M)	19	(F)
Lesbian & Gay Task Force (1988)	Pennsylvania	1987	28	(M)	25	(F)
Levine and Leonard (1984)	New York City	1980-1981	–		24	(F)
San Francisco Examiner,	National	1989	18	(M)	13	(F)
Teichner	Bay Area	1989	27	(M)	36	(F)
National Gay & Lesbian Task Force	National	1991	62	(M)	59	(F)

Note: Discrimination rate cross-tabulated by sex where possible.

Another way that economists and sociologists have documented discrimination against women and people of color involves comparing similar individuals to look for the impact of discrimination in lower income groups. Economic data on lesbians and gay men is difficult to find, not surprisingly. In the nonrandom surveys in which income and other economic data were collected, respondents tended to be disproportionately white, urban, and well-educated, all factors that raise average income, causing what statisticians call "sample selection bias." This bias makes inferences about the incomes of the larger population of lesbian and gay people inaccurate, such as the one cited earlier from the Colorado pamphlet.

Table 5 presents income figures from three recent national surveys of lesbian, gay, and bisexual people and compares those figures to national medians or averages. Without controlling for age or education, comparisons with the national medians may be misleading, especially given the likely sample selection bias. But even the survey with the least biased sampling technique (Teichner/*San Francisco Examiner*) resulted in high median incomes, especially for women and people of color (although small sample sizes probably explain most of the apparent difference for people of color). The crude comparisons of income by sexual orientation are quite

TABLE 5. Income of Lesbian, Gay, or Bisexual People

Survey	Instrument	Sample	Lesbian/ Gay/ Bisexual Income	National Income*
Out/Look (1988)	Magazine survey, mail-in	510	(Range for median)	
			Men 25K-29K	27,342
			Women 20K-24K	18,823
Simmons Market Research Bureau (1988)	Gay newspaper inserts		36,900 (Average individual) 55,430 (Average household)	
Teichner/ San Francisco Examiner (1989, n = 400)	Phone survey, Random digit dialing		(Median)	
			Men 29,129	28,605
			Women 26,331	19,643
			White** 28,266	29,846
			Black** 32,503	20,706
			Hisp.** 26,666	
			Asian** 30,012	

* "National income" is median income for full-time, full-year workers.
** Medians by race are for men only.
Sources: L/G/B incomes from unpublished data from each survey.
National medians from *Economic Report of the President* (1990, 1991).

different from simple cross-race or cross-gender comparisons, which usually show large differences. The lack of dramatic disparities by sexual orientation does not mean that discrimination does not exist, but rather that sexual orientation might not have the same labor market effects that race and sex do.

A common statistical approach for capturing the effects of discrimination is to see if people who are similar in all observable and economically relevant ways have similar labor market outcomes.[8] If income varies with non-productive characteristics such as race or gender among otherwise identical individuals, then researchers infer the existence of discrimination. I recently conducted such a study with data from the General Social Survey, a national random sample, which allows identification of behaviorally lesbian, gay, and bisexual individuals (Badgett, 1994). Unlike the studies in Table 5, in this sample the behaviorally gay sample has a lower average income even before controlling for education, age, etc., and the income disadvantage remains after using such controls, although the difference is not statistically significant for lesbians.

Unfortunately, the data do not include information about either sexual identity or workplace disclosure, making this finding an imperfect measure–probably an underestimate–of the effects of discrimination. One of the greatest challenges in research on sexual orientation is collecting appropriate data for statistical analysis. The most difficult question for survey design concerns disclosure of a gay or bisexual orientation to the interviewer. What question should a researcher ask? If either behavior or identity can lead to sanctions, then the prudent researcher will ask about both: not all people who engage in same-sex sexual activity consider themselves gay, lesbian, or even bisexual, and not all people who consider themselves gay or lesbian engage in sexual activity at all. A multi-question approach including behavior as well as identity would also avoid the potential cultural bias discussed earlier.

Careful construction of questions and use of both written and verbal response methods, appropriate selection of interviewers, and sensitivity to the concerns of interviewees will increase the reliability of responses. One way of assessing reliability that would also allow some modelling of the disclosure process would be to do in-depth follow-up interviews on a subsample. Recent advancements in statistical techniques have allowed social science statisticians to remove some of the effects of sample selection bias as well as to analyze longitudinal data[9] and many subtly different decision-making processes.[10] While getting a representative sample will be difficult given the relative paucity of research on this topic, the usefulness of econometric models requires the information that such an effort could provide.

Two other research strategies, workplace case studies and matched pair testing, offer less costly data collection. Case studies allow greater institutional and personal detail and have an added advantage of allowing an examination of an important assumption, i.e., that a lesbian, gay, or bisexual employee's disclosure is perceived correctly by coworkers or employers. And depending on the workplace studied, the researcher may also be able to study the effects of gay employee groups on disclosure and discrimination.

Matched pair testing is most useful in studying the job application process and involves sending out pairs of applicants or applications that are matched in all basic characteristics–age, education, etc.–except for the characteristic being tested (Turner, Fix, & Struyk, 1991). This technique has the advantage of controlling for all other relevant variables by construction, including disclosure. (In fact, the testers' actual sexual orientation would be irrelevant in this kind of study.) Adam (1981) used a similar technique to measure discrimination against lesbian and gay Canadian law students who were seeking post-schooling internships: gay-labelled resumes (those with a line "Active in [local] Gay People's Alliance") generated fewer interview offers than identical resumes that were not so labelled. One issue in a larger study is to avoid confounding an employer's bias against lesbians or gay men with an employer's bias against people in political organizations (as the Adams study may have done). Nevertheless, it should be possible to come up with an innocuous sounding organization (Lesbian and Gay Square Dancers, for instance) that keeps the difference between applicants focused on sexual orientation alone.

These suggestions for research show that quantitative studies of sexual orientation and employment discrimination are possible. Combining the results of that research with existing and future qualitative work, such as that done by Woods (1993) and by Hall (1989), will contribute to a more complete understanding of the labor market position of, and discrimination against, lesbian, gay, and bisexual workers. And while we may now know enough about the existence of discrimination to conclude that federal policy should prohibit discrimination because of sexual orientation, a more detailed and sensitive research methodology is necessary to address other policy concerns, such as enforcement, monitoring, and affirmative action.

For lesbian/gay/bisexual workplace groups, results of research on disclosure and discrimination will, first of all, help them to understand the forces working to keep gay people in the closet at work, a situation that can be frustrating to gay workers who are out and are actively seeking changes in the workplace. Second, research will help both gay workers and the helping professionals who work with gay workers to identify potential points of discrimination: are gay workers more vulnerable during the hiring process? in everyday interactions with supervisors and coworkers? in promotions? In addition, research can demonstrate to employers that discrimination is costly, whether indirect (from keeping workers in the closet) or direct (from losing productive workers), supporting both personnel managers and gay workers in their efforts to change employment policies.

In direct interactions with individual lesbian, gay, or bisexual workers, personnel managers and counselors must understand the significance of gay workers having no legal protection from discrimination as well as the double or triple jeopardy faced by lesbians and gay people of color. Promoting gay workers' psychological and economic health requires a nuanced consideration of the constraints and incentives involved in managing a gay or bisexual identity at work. With that understanding, helping professionals can work to minimize the risk of discrimination while allowing lesbian, gay, and bisexual workers to find a level of disclosure that is both personally comfortable and functional.

NOTES

1. Some state courts have interpreted state civil rights codes to include sexual orientation (e.g., *Gay Law Students Associations v. Pacific Telephone and Telegraph Co.*).

2. For instance, Moore, 1993, shows the number of people who believe that homosexuals should have equal job opportunities rose from 56% to 80% between 1977 and 1993.

3. Although race is considered easily "observable," to say that race is observable by defining it in purely physical terms is an elusive and increasingly mistaken venture. For instance, some light-skinned black people have passed as white in the United States to avoid discrimination (Omi & Winant, 1986). A related concept, ethnicity, also involves an important social dimension in its construction. (For further discussion of the social and political nature of racial and ethnic identity, see Omi & Winant, 1986.) Gender's connection to the biologically based categories of sex makes its physical observability somewhat less problematic. In a functional sense, the "observability" of these characteristics refers to an observer's ability to infer the characteristics of race, ethnicity, and gender and an individual's willingness to reveal those characteristics consistently.

4. In its wide range of uses, the term "sexual orientation" refers either to behavior or to identity.

5. Disclosure is not necessarily a binary concept–being either in or out of the closet. Woods's study of how gay men manage their sexual identities in their professional lives reveals three main strategies (Woods, 1993). Two of them, "counterfeiting" a heterosexual identity and "avoidance" of topics related to sexual identity, clearly lead to a low degree of disclosure to coworkers. But at least some men using those strategies do reveal their sexual identity to carefully selected coworkers, although under the general assumption of confidentiality. The third strategy, "integration" of a gay identity within the workplace, is a much more disclosive strategy. In the context of this framework, then, "disclosure" could refer to a disclosive strategy involving relative openness about one's sexual identity.

6. Reviews of other similar surveys showing comparable discrimination rates can be found in Badgett, Donnelly, and Kibbe, 1992; Levine, 1980; Levine and Leonard, 1984.

7. The Teichner/*San Francisco Examiner* poll is an exception, using random digit dialing to find lesbian, gay, and bisexual people.

8. Typically, researchers use ordinary least squares procedures to determine the relationship between income and the explanatory variables, such as age, education, occupation, race, and gender.

9. Longitudinal data (data collected on the same individuals over time) would allow comparisons of labor market outcomes before and after disclosure for an individual and comparisons with the experience of nondisclosing or straight workers.

10. For instance, the disclosure to come out could be modelled statistically in what is known as a switching regressions model: a lesbian worker chooses between a potentially low income path (if she discloses her sexual orientation and faces discrimination) and a high income path (from passing), with her decision based partly on the likely difference in incomes. For a review of this and other techniques, see Maddala, 1983.

REFERENCES

Adam, B. D. (1981). Stigma and employability: Discrimination by sex and sexual orientation in the Ontario legal profession. *Canadian Review of Sociology and Anthropology, 18,* 216-221.

Alonso, A. M., & Koreck, M. T. (1989). Silences: 'Hispanics', AIDS, and sexual practices. *Differences, 1,* 101-124.

American Civil Liberties Union. (1991). Lesbian and Gay Rights Project.

Badgett, M. V. L. (1994). The wage effect of sexual orientation discrimination. *Industrial and Labor Relations Review,* forthcoming.

Badgett, L., Donnelly, C., & Kibbe, J. (1992). Pervasive patterns of discrimination against lesbians and gay men: Evidence from surveys across the United States. National Gay and Lesbian Task Force Policy Institute.

Badgett, M. V. L., & Williams, R. M. (1992). The economics of sexual orientation: Establishing a research agenda. *Feminist Studies, 18*, 649-657.

Bergmann, B. R. (1989). Does the market for women's labor need fixing? *Journal of Economic Perspectives, 3*, 43-60.

Blau, F. D., & Beller, A. H. (1992). Black-White earnings over the 1970s and 1980s: Gender differences in trends. *Review of Economics and Statistics, 74*, 276-286.

Brause, J. (1989). Closed doors: Sexual orientation bias in the Anchorage housing and employment markets. In *Identity reports: Sexual orientation bias in Alaska*. Anchorage, AK: Identity Incorporated.

Building Community at PG&E. (1992). *The gay/lesbian/bisexual corporate letter, 1*, 3-6.

Carlson, L. A., & Swartz, C. (1988). The earnings of women and ethnic minorities, 1959-1979. *Industrial and Labor Relations Review, 41*, 530-552.

Colorado for Family Values (1992). Stop special class status for homosexuality.

Economic report of the president. (1990). Washington, DC: U.S. Government Printing Office.

Economic report of the president. (1991). Washington, DC: U.S. Government Printing Office.

Editors of *Harvard Law Review*. (1991). *Sexual orientation and the law*. Cambridge, MA: Harvard University Press.

Escoffier, J. (1975). Stigmas, work environment, and economic discrimination against homosexuals. *Homosexual Counseling Journal, 2*, 8-17.

Garnets, L., & Kimmel, D. (1991). Lesbian and gay male dimensions in the psychological study of human diversity. In J. D. Goodchilds (Ed.), *Psychological perspectives on human diversity in America*. Washington, DC: American Psychological Association.

Hall, M. (1989). Private experiences in the public domain: Lesbians in organizations. In J. Hearn, D. L. Sheppard, P. Tancred-Sherrif, & G. Burrell (Eds.), *The sexuality of organization* (pp. 125-138). London: Sage Publications.

Herek, G. (1991). Stigma, prejudice, and violence against lesbians and gay men. In J. C. Gonsiorek & J. D. Weinrich (Eds.), *Homosexuality: Research implications for public policy* (pp. 60-80). Newbury Park: Sage Publications.

King, M. (1992). Occupational segregation by race and sex, 1940-88. *Monthly Labor Review, 115*, 30-37.

Levine, M. (1980). Employment discrimination against gay men. In J. Harry and M. S. Das (Eds.), *Homosexuality in international perspective*. Vikas Publishing House.

Levine, M., & Leonard, R. (1984). Discrimination against lesbians in the work force. *Signs, 9*, 700-710.

Maddala G. S. (1983). Limited dependent and qualitative variables in econometrics. *Econometric Society Monographs No. 3*. Cambridge: Cambridge University Press.

Martinez, M. N. (1993). Recognizing sexual orientation is fair and not costly. *HR Magazine*, June, 66-72.

Matthaei, J. (1993). The sexual division of labor, sexuality, and lesbian/gay liberation: Towards a marxist-feminist analysis of sexuality in U.S. capitalism. *Review of Radical Political Economics*, forthcoming.

Mohr, R. (1988). *Gays/Justice: A study of ethics, society, and law.* New York, NY: Columbia University Press.

Moore, D. W. (1993). Public polarized on gay issue. *The Gallup Poll Monthly*, 331, April, 30-34.

Omi, M., & Winant, H. (1986). *Racial formation in the United States.* New York: Routledge.

Posner, R. (1992). *Sex and reason.* Cambridge: Harvard University Press.

Rubenstein, W. B. (Ed.) (1993). *Lesbians, gay men, and the law.* New York: The New Press.

Schneider, B. (1986). Coming out at work: Bridging the private/public gap. *Work and Occupations, 13,* 463-487.

Shao, M., with Dawley, H. (1991). The right to privacy: A $5.3 million lesson for Shell? *Business Week,* August 26.

Ten Percent (1993). Why we need a federal civil rights law. Fall, 29.

Turner, M. A., Fix, M., & Struyk, R. J. (1991). *Opportunities denied, opportunities diminished: Racial discrimination in hiring.* Washington, DC: The Urban Institute Press.

Woods, J. D., with Lucas, J. H. (1993). *The corporate closet: The professional lives of gay men in America.* New York: The Free Press.

Domestic Partner Benefits:
A Bottom Line Discussion

Sue Spielman
Liz Winfeld

SUMMARY. More and more organizations, including businesses, universities and municipalities, are being faced with requests from their employees to implement domestic partner benefits (including medical coverage). The questions that these requests raise cover the entire spectrum from the concrete to the philosophical. This article includes discussion of the following topics: should organizations have a non-discrimination policy inclusive of sexual orientation; how to find out how much medical benefits for domestic partners will cost; where to find an insurer to cover domestic partners; whether these benefits should be offered to both heterosexual and homosexual couples; how to define a "domestic partner"; what laws and tax codes govern these benefits; and, how to communicate changes in benefit plans to employees. These, and many other topics, demand the attention of human resources professionals. *[Article copies available from The Haworth Document Delivery Service: 1-800-342-9678.]*

Sue Spielman, MS, and Liz Winfeld, MA, are founders of and consultants for Common Ground, a training/consulting firm specializing in gay/lesbian issues in the workplace, domestic partner benefits, and AIDS/HIV and STD workplace education.

Address correspondence to Liz Winfeld at Common Ground, 10 Home Avenue, Natick, MA 01760.

[Haworth co-indexing entry note]: "Domestic Partner Benefits: A Bottom Line Discussion." Spielman, Sue, and Liz Winfeld. Co-published simultaneously in *Journal of Gay & Lesbian Social Services* (The Haworth Press, Inc.) Vol. 4, No. 4, 1996, pp. 53-78; and: *Sexual Identity on the Job: Issues and Services* (ed: Alan L. Ellis, and Ellen D. B. Riggle) The Haworth Press, Inc., 1996, pp. 53-78; and: *Sexual Identity on the Job: Issues and Services* (ed: Alan L. Ellis, and Ellen D. B. Riggle) Harrington Park Press, an imprint of The Haworth Press, Inc., 1996, pp. 53-78. Single or multiple copies of this article are available from The Haworth Document Delivery Service [1-800-342-9678, 9:00 a.m. - 5:00 p.m. (EST)].

© 1996 by The Haworth Press, Inc. All rights reserved.

53

INTRODUCTION

This article will present an argument that the provision by employers of domestic partner benefits to their gay/lesbian employees is an issue that transcends simple matters of fairness or personal beliefs about sexual orientation. It will also explain what these benefits are, who they serve, and how they can and should be implemented.

In the 1990s, employers bear the burden—or enjoy the opportunity—to influence the behavior and affect the well-being of each employee beyond any degree of influence ever experienced before. Therefore, questions such as those related and intrinsic to domestic partner benefits are of vital importance to all employers today and for the future.

A Brief History

Domestic partner benefits are frequently thought of in relation to the workplace sector—public entities, private corporations, or institutions of learning—in which they are offered. The types of workplace perquisites in each of these sectors can differ slightly, but the sector continues to matter only in terms of the machinations that an individual or group must go through in order to see to their implementation. The benefits themselves, and most issues related to them, are basically the same.

The Village Voice in New York first extended benefits to what they called "spousal equivalents" in 1982 as a result of a negotiation with one of its labor unions. The American Psychological Association Insurance Trust extended benefits in 1983. The City of Berkeley extended benefits in 1985 and was quickly followed by Santa Cruz, San Francisco, West Hollywood, Laguna Beach, and Seattle (Van Sluys, 1991). Cambridge, Massachusetts was the first non-West Coast city to implement the benefits. Ben and Jerry's of Vermont climbed on the bandwagon in 1989, and they were followed in turn by Montefiore Medical Center and Lotus, both in 1991. Stanford University, Columbia University, the University of Minnesota and the University of Iowa were the first institutions of higher learning to incorporate the benefits, all between 1990 and 1991.

In short, between 1990 and 1994, the number of businesses, universities, and municipalities that have chosen to offer domestic partner benefits inclusive of medical benefits has increased from under five (5) to over 130. And the number that offer employee benefits exclusive of medical coverage is close to three times that number (Winfeld & Spielman, 1995).

While these numbers do not represent an avalanche, the movement towards the extension of these benefits is gaining momentum. There are two reasons for this. The first (more philosophical) reason that companies are extending the benefits is because they believe that it is the right thing to do. The second (more practical) reason is that they are implementing the benefits to gain or maintain a competitive edge.

Microsoft is a good example of both reasons at work. A basic operating principle of this technological company is to seek out and leverage the differing needs and backgrounds of their employees. Microsoft recognizes that if they are to achieve their goal of putting a computer on every desktop in every home, they have to know who those people sitting at those desktops are and what they are like. A company that values diversity will make sure its products are accessible to people from all walks of life, and they will actively recruit people of diverse backgrounds and implement programs to take care of them. Microsoft has specifically tracked how much it costs to attract, train, and keep employees, and they consider turnover to be prohibitively expensive. According to their own study, they believe that each lost employee represents two million dollars in lost revenue for the company over time. Similarly, it has been well documented that every time the U.S. military discharges an enlisted person or officer for homosexuality, it costs them $27,000 and $120,000 respectively for each discharged person (Conahan, 1992).

Diversity is a major business advantage. It is the difference between limiting a company or institution to a single cultural value and achieving fullness and wholeness by welcoming difference. Organizations are faced with the reality that their workforces will continue to become more diverse. For example, about 45% of all net additions to the labor force in the 1990s will be non-white; by the year 2000, the majority of public school-age children will be non-white. As time goes on, more organizations will be faced with requests from their employees to implement benefits reflective of a more diverse workforce (American Civil Liberties Union, 1992).

ORGANIZATIONAL ATTITUDES

When we consider how people form attitudes, at least as far as the scope of the workplace is concerned, it is believed that we do so in layers: first as individuals, then as part of a specific group, and last as part of an organization which has a great deal of influence over how we, as individuals, actually feel about things.

The term "organizational culture" has been defined as the "underlying values, beliefs, and principles that serve as a foundation for the organization's management system, as well as the set of management practices and behaviors that both exemplify and reinforce those principles" (Cox, 1993). Organizational socialization is the process by which individuals adopt, to a greater or lesser degree, the values, abilities, expected behaviors and social knowledge essential for assuming a role and for participating as an accepted member of the organization (Cox, 1993). In other words, everyone seeks to fit in, and the degree to which we do or do not fit in affects our performance.

If we are talking about culture and socialization of minorities into the majority in order to form a working organization, gays are different enough to warrant our own grouping if only because we enter every situation with a different set of norms than the heterosexual majority does. ["Gays" is meant to be inclusive of gay women and men, and where applicable, bisexuals.] Group identities, the norms with which we enter any situation, have a significant influence on our worldview. When a group has held a dominant position in a social system over a long period of time, members of the group experience psychological discomfort when the percentage of minority members is perceived to be greater than the majority, even when there is still no chance of the majority being outnumbered (Davis, 1985). The work done by Davis and others explains to a large degree why members of minority groups often lobby organizations to increase the representation of their culture group in the organization, while members of the majority group often resist these efforts.

How this affects the workplace relative to gays and their desires to seek equitable work-related benefits draws one into a discussion of what has been labeled the "asexual imperative" (Woods, 1993). That is, as a society we agree that the workplace should be an asexual environment; the reality is that it is anything but. Professional relationships are based on social ones, and social relationships are often founded on the exchange of personal information and opinions that are anything but asexual. Heterosexuals can freely put a picture of the "spouse and kids" on their desks without being accused of bringing their "sex life" to work. However, if their gay counterparts display a picture of their partner, they would be accused of flaunting their sex life.

The reason for mentioning the asexual imperative is to highlight the point that people bring their personal lives to work in the form of pictures or banter around the coffee machine because it is our personal lives, and the people in them, that motivate us to succeed. Therefore, we (gays and straights) hold our partners and families to be of the utmost importance, and we want benefits that will protect them.

CHANGE IN THE WORKPLACE

In mid-1994, a poll was released by Time/CNN indicating that 52% of Americans consider the so-called "gay-lifestyle" acceptable, a percentage that reflects an increase from just 35% in April 1976 (*Time*, 1994). A majority of the people surveyed also believed that gays should be able to get medical benefits from their employer or partner's employer, and that the new health care system in this country should make provisions for gay/lesbian households. However, in the same poll, 64% said they do not think gay marriages should be recognized by law, and 45% say laws protecting the civil rights of racial or religious minorities should not apply to gays (*Time*, 1994). In a 1994 *Newsweek* poll, the majority surveyed opposed legally-sanctioned adoption rights for gay or lesbian couples, but over 70% favored gay job and housing rights (*Newsweek*, 1994).

These are fascinating juxtapositions of opinion, and we believe that there is a reason for them. Every time gay people set forth a requirement for equal treatment that is directly related to the nature of our relationships, we challenge the myth and the idea of the "traditional American family." The definition of the traditional American family is a wage-earner husband, his wife, and their two children under eighteen, all living under the same roof. This construct of the American family being in the majority has not existed since pre-World War II, and it has always been an extremely hard model to find among the poor and working class, where often both parents have to work. The wife was, and is, almost never afforded the "luxury" (or opportunity) of being a full-time homemaker.

FAMILY DEFINITIONS

The U.S. Census Bureau's 1990 Information Survey of 57,000 American homes revealed that in that year, seventy-five percent (75%) or three-quarters of all American families were non-traditional (U.S. Census Bureau, 1990). In the Bureau's 1994 annual analysis of households, families defined as two or more persons related by birth, marriage, and/or adoption and residing together, comprised seventy-one percent of all households, down from eighty-one percent in 1970. Accompanying the decline of the traditional family during the years 1970-1992 has been the 400% increase in domestic partnerships in the U.S. As of 1992, there were 4.5 million such partnerships according to the Census Bureau, of which 3 million were heterosexual couples and 1.5 million self-identified as homosexual partnerships.

A significant comment issued along with the Census Bureau's 1994 Report was that "one would be hard-pressed to find families that merit the description *typical* in today's United States" (U.S. Census Bureau, 1994). In an effort to better define the family, the Bureau's Marriage and Family Division expected to release a report in the summer of 1995 which would attempt to give a more accurate account of all family structures, including domestic partnerships of both same-sex and opposite-sex partners. But all evidence points to the fact that non-traditional families so outnumber traditional groupings that the definition of "family" is only going to get harder to pinpoint as time goes on.

In 1989, Mass Mutual Life Insurance Company conducted an "American Families Value Study" (Mass Mutual Life, 1989). In that study, nearly three-quarters of the respondents defined the family in structural or emotional terms rather than by legal definition. The most common definition of a family was "a group who love and care for each other." According to Mass Mutual's study, family values are love and emotional support, respect for others, and taking responsibility for one's own actions. This study indicates that the way people define family values transcends sexual orientation, and yet because of the myth of the "traditional family," people have a difficult time acknowledging that a same-sex couple, with or without biological or adoptive children, can be an effective, loving, and nurturing family unit.

The above cited public opinions, along with conceptions of the traditional family and misconceptions about non-traditional families are at the crux of why the battle for gay rights is being fought in the workplace, and why a main focus of the battle is benefits. The workforce comes from the forces shaping the family. It is logical to conclude that if three-quarters or more of all American families fit a non-traditional model, then at least three-quarters of all workers are bringing new and different preconceptions and requirements into the workplace. It is also logical to conclude that the markets into which products and services are being sold are similarly non-traditional.

WORKPLACE POLICIES AND BENEFITS

Since the early 1980s about two dozen studies have sought to document hiring, promotion, and compensation practices that discriminate against lesbian and gay workers. According to the U.S. Chamber of Commerce (American Civil Liberties Union, 1992) employee benefits like health insurance, relocation expense reimbursement, and other perquisites can account for up to 37-40% of an individual's compensation. If these benefits are only going to straight employees, why would qualified gays or lesbians work where they will be treated like second class citizens?

Suppose you have a worker named Suzanne whose partner, Jenny, is a freelance writer with no health insurance. Suzanne shares a workspace with Lisa whose husband, Ed, is also a freelance writer, but who is covered in full for health and dental benefits under Suzanne and Lisa's company plan. Suzanne knows that Lisa's life-partner, her legal spouse, is covered, while her own life-partner is not. This makes her resentful towards the company and towards Lisa, although she probably never demonstrates it overtly. Her resentment is manifested, however, in a lack of enthusiasm for the company and her job. It affects her ability to give her all to the team, which ultimately affects the performance of the entire organization.

So what is it that gay and lesbian people really want from the workplace that will help them to be the best performers they can be? Brian McNaught, in his book *Gay Issues in the Workplace* (1993), describes the seven items that gays and lesbians want:

1. a specific employment policy that prohibits discrimination based on sexual orientation;
2. creation of a safe work environment that is free of heterosexist, homophobic, and AIDS-phobic behaviors;
3. company-wide education about gay issues in the workplace and AIDS;
4. an equitable benefits program that recognizes domestic partners of gay, lesbian and bisexual employees;
5. freedom for all employees to participate fully in all aspects of corporate life;
6. support of gay/lesbian/bisexual employee support groups; and
7. public support of gay issues.

The remainder of this article will focus on equitable benefits and specific non-discrimination policies.

Benefits

We have already explained why these benefits are vital to the happiness and productivity of gay/lesbian workers. We will now address specifically what is involved in these benefits and how they can and must be implemented. It is within the "how to implement" discussion that we will address in detail the question of non-discrimination policies.

Benefits that can be awarded to employees by employers fall into two general categories: soft benefits and hard benefits.

Soft benefits are those which, while certainly costing money, are not considered to be as cost intensive. To a certain extent, soft benefits have to be considered in terms of the sector within which the organization falls. For instance, in the private sector, soft benefits might include: adoption benefits, bereavement and family leave, employee assistance program eligibility, parenting leave, use of health and fitness facilities, relocation assistance for an employee and his/her family, and sick leave. In the public sector (i.e., within states or municipalities), some of the above may apply, but there could be other partner benefits, such as: registration of domestic partnership, use of recreational areas, or visitation rights in hospitals or prisons. Finally, in the college/university sector, faculty/staff privileges, student/faculty housing, or a university ID card might be thrown into the mix.

Hard benefits are commonly thought of as "cost intensive." These include medical, dental, and pension benefits. Hard benefits do not include life insurance because all fifty U.S. states prohibit unmarried partners from being party to employee-sponsored group life insurance. With this exception, employers may at their discretion, offer any benefit to any employee, partner, or family member as the organization defines these terms.

What defines a domestic partner? Loralie Van Sluys (1991) of Hewitt Associates in Chicago gathered the following definitions and terms:

1. A relationship resembling a family or household with close cooperation between the parties, each having specified responsibilities.
2. A committed, nonplatonic, family-type relationship of two unrelated partners.
3. Two unrelated individuals who share the necessities of life, live together, and have an emotional and financial commitment to one another.
4. Two individuals who have an intimate and committed relationship, and are jointly responsible for basic living expenses.
5. Terms such as cohabitant, significant other, spousal equivalent, nontraditional dependent, or live-in companion.

Columbia University defines domestic partners as ". . . two individuals of the same gender who live together in a long-term relationship of infinite duration, with an exclusive mutual commitment similar to that of marriage, in which the partners agree to be financially responsible for each other's welfare and share financial obligations" (Columbia University, 1993). This definition is used to determine the criteria for which benefits are granted to the partners of employees at Columbia. Specifically, Columbia and its insurers have been known to ask for some of the following specific proofs that a relationship meets their definition:

1. to be of the same sex and not married;
2. to have lived together for at least six months and intend to do so indefinitely;
3. to meet the age and mental competency requirements for marriage in the State of New York;
4. to not be related by blood to a degree of closeness that would prohibit legal marriage in the state of legal residence;
5. to be jointly responsible for each other's common welfare and share financial obligations as demonstrated by three of the following:
    (a) domestic partner agreement where registration is available,
    (b) a joint mortgage or lease, designation of the partner as beneficiary of life insurance and retirement benefits,
    (c) designation of partner as primary beneficiary of a will,
    (d) assignment of durable property or health care proxy to the partner,
    (e) joint ownership of a car, bank account, or joint credit account.

The burden of proof for same-sex couples exceeds that of opposite-sex couples. In most places, should a domestic partnership dissolve, both parties must notify the employee in writing as to the dissolution of the relationship. And in most cases, the employee would not be able to sign on another partner for at least six months. This, again, is not true in straight relationships where a woman can get a divorce one day, marry someone else the next, and that new spouse would be automatically entitled to his new wife's assets, benefits, property, etc.

It is important to note that while it is overwhelmingly a gay/lesbian employee who will petition for the implementation of these benefits, it is overwhelmingly straight unmarried couples who will take advantage of them if they can. The reasons for this are simple. First, most two-adult gay/lesbian relationships consist of parties who work and who are insured by their own employer. Second, it can be difficult to meet the requirements of partnership. Third, gay people may not want to run the risk of "outing" themselves by electing the benefits.

Overcoming Objections to Domestic Partner Benefits

There are relatively standard objections to domestic partner benefits for same-sex couples. Many employers object to implementing these benefits on the grounds that the on-going national health care debate, and the concept of "universal coverage" will solve all these problems. But this is not the case given the current plans under debate. Also, even if the plans under debate made any provisions at all for partner medical coverage (which they do not) they do not even remotely address those benefits classified as "soft." According to the Segal Corporation (Sherman, 1993), the future of domestic partner benefits offered by employers will be thrown into more doubt, not less, by universal coverage plans.

None of the plans, for instance, attempt to define the term "spouse," leaving such definition in the hands of individual states. Universal coverage is one thing; who is going to pay for each person's coverage is quite another. For instance, under certain proposals, a non-insured, self-employed or unemployed domestic partner of an employee would have to pay 100% of his or her premium, whereas the spouse of another employee at the same company would be covered up to 80% by the employer. These proposals also state that the employer can pay up to 100% of the cost of individual or family coverage, but are silent as to whether that family coverage would include a partner. The proposals are also silent on the question of imputed income and tax on benefits (Sherman, 1993).

According to the National Gay and Lesbian Task Force, these plans discriminate financially against non-traditional families by defining a family as a married couple or a single person with children. A gay couple with a child and big health bills could pay $4500 in deductibles as compared with $3000 for the traditional family. Therefore, using the eventual resolution of the health care debate as an excuse not to implement benefits for the partners of gay/lesbian employees is not a legitimate argument.

The next objection is usually cost, and objections based on cost are often veiled instances of AIDS-phobia. The first thing to understand about domestic partner benefits relative to cost is that by instituting them, you are not introducing a new benefit, you are simply extending existing benefits. And contrary to fears and warnings propagated to a large extent by the insurance industry in the late 1980s, extending coverage to domestic partners has not resulted in increased cost due to adverse selection. Experience from 1985 to the present indicates that employers are at no more risk when adding domestic partners than when adding spouses to policies.

Apple Corporation issued a study in the third quarter of 1992. Using themselves, Lotus, Seattle, Berkeley, Montefiore and other organizations as a basis, they determined that when benefits were implemented for same-sex partners only, the average cost increase to the issuing enterprise was 0.4% to 0.7%. When these benefits were implemented for heterosexual couples as well, the average increase in cost was 3.4%. At Lotus, by the end of 1993, out of 4000 employees, only sixteen same-sex couples had elected these benefits; at Apple, out of 9000, 45 employees in same-sex partnerships signed up. These low rates translate into low costs.

Second, a proliferation of AIDS claims has never materialized. AIDS is not a gay disease and not all gay men are AIDS-afflicted. In fact, the majority of gay men are not HIV+. Lesbians remain in the lowest risk group for HIV infection.

The average cost for AIDS treatment, for the lifetime of an AIDS-infected individual, is roughly $70,000, with the highest estimate at $115,000. This higher figure occurred after the CDC expanded its definition of AIDS affliction (National Leadership Coalition on AIDS, 1993). Compare this figure to birth related expenses which start at $70,000 in cases of premature birth. Just two weeks of intensive care after a heart attack can cost $50-$70,000, while cancer averages $30,000 to over $100,000 (National Leadership Coalition on AIDS, 1993).

AIDS, while certainly physically and emotionally devastating, ranks at least fourth behind these other conditions in terms of cost. And while AIDS has the potential to be an enormous drain on the future of health insurance and health care, it is not because gays and lesbians are getting sick, but rather because more heterosexuals are becoming infected.

Another cost concern is surcharges on domestic partner plans set by insurance companies. But, since 1985, every municipality, university, or company asked by their insurance company to pay an additional surcharge for domestic partner coverage at inception of the plan, has had those surcharges revoked within two years of implementation because they were not, in any case, justified (Apple Corporation, 1992).

Enrollment objections revolve around two questions: whether or not to include same-sex couples only and how to protect the organization from fraud. As noted before, even though it is gay/lesbian employees who will usually fight for these benefits, it is straight employees who will sign up for them if they can. And by including straight couples in the policy, companies are almost guaranteeing their costs will go up more because of the likelihood that heterosexual couples, married or not, will at some point incur birth related expenses. As more and more gay and lesbian couples opt for children, these numbers may come into balance. But for now, straight partners are more expensive than gay partners.

Fraud fears are also a thinly disguised AIDS-related and homophobic bias. It was feared that any gay person would sign up any gay friend, partner or not, to get that person coverage if they were HIV-afflicted. In fact, prior to enacting their benefits, San Francisco endeavored to find out if they were already covering people fraudulently, and found that they were. One percent of the City's enrollees were enrolled fraudulently, every one a heterosexual claiming to be legally married to the person on his/her insurance (University of Iowa, 1991).

The affidavits required by nearly 100% of all enterprises offering these benefits have proven to be very effective fraud deterrents. Falsifying such documentation can result in job loss. Also, the tax ramifications of accepting partner benefits are real and considerable to the employee. It is not an arrangement to enter into lightly, and few have.

When considering using cost-based arguments as objections to implementing domestic partner benefits, the organization should also consider the various alternatives available to them. Although we advocate for equal benefits in every sense, some other measures might work better in some situations. The enterprise can, for instance, investigate whether to offer benefits that exclude a partner's dependents; whether to split premiums with the employee, or offer other cash incentives to offset costs and/or taxes; whether to offer the employee cash in lieu of coverage entirely; or whether simply to provide administrative services and not offer any financial assistance at all. All of these options have been used in all sectors.

Another option is to offer a plan consisting of "benefits credits" in which each employee is granted a number of credits that can be redeemed for any benefit the company offers across the board. For instance, a single parent with a child could opt to use some credits for daycare; a single person with no dependents could use the credits towards a health club membership, and gay employees could use the credits to provide medical insurance for their partners.

One last objection that must be addressed is when companies decline to offer partner benefits because they claim that if they do so, they will have to cover employee's aunts, uncles, parents, nieces, etc. Right now, employment benefits are directly tied to marital and legal dependent status. In the U.S., one does not automatically qualify for anything–benefits, pensions, insurance proceeds, visitation rights, anything–without some proof of being a spouse or a legal dependent. Therefore, companies by virtue of offering insurance to legal spouses and dependents now are not in any way bound to cover an employee's parents, grandparents, siblings or anyone else. Offering partner benefits will likewise not make such coverage an inevitable conclusion. Gay and lesbian people are seeking equality only; they are not seeking anything that their heterosexual counterparts do not enjoy by virtue of legal marriage. The only thing that will reduce the cry for domestic partner benefits will be the legalization and validation of gay/lesbian life-partnerships.

Insurance Companies and Plans

Next comes the question of how the insurance companies currently address all of this. In almost every instance when organizations have looked at implementing these benefits but decided against it, they have usually cast their insurance company in the villain's role. This may not be fair or even true. Homophobia should usually be cast in that dark role. At this time, it's probably more accurate to say that insurers are guilty of not looking at the actual numbers or historical data, and are not willing to take a leadership position in the implementation of these benefits. However, a lot of progress has been made in the last ten years.

When the City of West Hollywood first sought insurers in 1984 and 1985, they were turned down by sixteen companies and were forced to turn to a plan of self-insurance augmented by stop-loss coverage (Van Sluys, 1991). To date, only Delta Dental will offer partner benefits to any group's domestic partners. The rest of the industry is coming along slowly but surely, but most still impose limitations and caveats to their coverage. Without a doubt, companies with fewer than five hundred employees are going to find it more difficult to get insurers and HMOs to cooperate, but it is getting easier every day.

A larger size insurance company gears itself towards groups of 500 or more; mid-range companies insure groups of 100-500 people; some companies specialize in small businesses and groups of fewer than 100. It is our opinion that most groups of fewer than 500 will have better luck with HMOs than with primary insurers because the HMOs are using domestic partner benefits as competitive leverage. Companies that serve the fewer than 500 arena typically purchase insured types of policies, where the company buys a fixed set of benefits for a fixed rate similar to homeowners or car insurance. Once beyond the 500 person threshold, it becomes more common for the employer to self-insure, whereby all claims submitted by employees are funded by a banking arrangement which reimburses the insurance company. In these arrangements, the insurance company is paid an administrative or management fee.

For companies with 5000 employees or more, the risk is so spread out that a pure self-insurance arrangement will usually generate enough revenue to fund the plan. But in groups of anywhere from 500-5000, stop-loss protection is usually purchased to protect the employer's assets from catastrophic claims. It is because of the need for stop-loss insurance that insurance companies can sometimes still complicate an employer's desire to implement the benefits. Again, this complication is usually due to a fear of AIDS. Employers who want to offer these benefits are faced with the task of deciding if they want to self-insure and to what extent, the amount of stop-loss protection to buy, and who will administer the plan.

One thing employers will find when they test the market is that increasingly, insurance companies are willing to make arrangements for stop-loss coverage and/or self insurance. Either arrangement can be entered into by an employer with a full service insurer, with a bank, or with an administrative overseer. Insurance companies operate in a competitive environment and realize that employers will most likely be able to get the coverage written the way they want it somewhere else. The insurance industry has not, to date, issued a list of companies that provide these sorts of plans. In our work, we have called every major insurer and found that while they do not advertise that they write these policies in an effort to maintain their client base, they rarely if ever turn them away. An employer only needs to ask and insist.

Pension Plans and Taxation

Gay/lesbian people cannot get married, and so do not enjoy the same automatic rights of survivorship or next-of-kin status that straight people do. Gay persons can write wills and name their partner as executor. Gays can give their partners durable power of attorney for all matters, and can make them the beneficiary of stock, private pension plans such as SEPs or KEOGHs, and can name them as the beneficiary of all life insurance. Health care proxies, giving the partner the right to make medical decisions should the person become incapacitated, are also available in some states, although it is not guaranteed that such a document will be honored.

But in the case where a pension plan is wholly company paid, gay domestic partners, and in fact, anyone who is not a legal spouse, can be denied payment upon the death of the employee. This is true as per legal precedent as decided in Rovira v. AT&T in 1993, where the Federal Court of Appeals agreed with the New Jersey State Courts in ruling that under ERISA (Employee Retirement Income Security Act) guidelines AT&T did not have to pay a deceased employee's pension to her partner of twelve years. Likewise, Hewlett Packard has recently changed its payout policy for retirement benefits such that only legal spouses can collect.

Therefore, if a company, even one that implements soft and hard benefits inclusive of medical/dental coverage, chooses to exclude pension benefits, chances are they can do so. However, they can also choose to pay them, as they can choose to offer COBRA (Continuation of Benefits Rights Act) benefits to partners similar to those offered to spouses/families of employees who leave the company.

Last is the issue of income tax. For employers, the tax ramifications of domestic partner benefits have become largely administrative. It has been commonly found through private letter rulings issued by the IRS at the request of various organizations, that the employer cost of domestic partner benefits is a compensation expense under IRS code section 162, attributable to the employment of the "employee partner." Therefore, the expense to the employer is not taxed, but it is also not a deductible expense, as it is for legal spouse benefits.

The tax obligation for employees who cover their partners is not as clear, and certainly not as favorable. When the City of Seattle requested an IRS opinion on the tax implications of these benefits to its employees, the IRS issued to them a response in the form of a private letter ruling (9034048) in May 1990. Since then, at least two other private letter rulings have been requested and issued, each agreeing with the original. According to the IRS, employer provided health benefits for domestic partners or non-spouse cohabitants of an employee are excludable from taxable income only if the recipients are legal spouses or legal dependents. For federal tax purposes, the determination of marital status is based on state law.

Dependent status is also dependent partially on state and local law, and the relationship must not violate local laws.

If the domestic partner is not a legal spouse and cannot qualify as a dependent under Section 152 of the IRS Code (which in 99.9% of all cases they cannot), then the fair market value of the employer provided benefits will be taxable under code sections 105 and 106. The fair market value is determined by a complex set of calculations which are best left to a paper devoted to such precise matters. Interesting variations on "partner," "spouse," and "dependent" arise in the case of Common Law marriage and adopted children. State common law marriage statutes typically give legal spouse status to heterosexual partners in the states where they are recognized. Pre-adoptive children do not qualify for benefits until they are legally adopted and are therefore considered legal dependents.

Non-Discrimination Policies

Once armed with all of the preceding information, the question remains: how to convince an employer to implement the benefits?

The first, most important action is to make sure that the company has in place a non-discrimination policy, and that sexual orientation is expressly included in that policy. It is not enough for a company to say "we don't discriminate on the basis of orientation." It must be written down for all to see, thereby leaving no doubt in the minds of gay/lesbian employees that they enjoy some measure of job protection, that their company is committed to equitable treatment, and leaving no doubt in the minds of less-than-tolerant coworkers that any form of abuse or harassment on the basis of orientation will not go unpunished.

Opponents of such job-related or civil rights provisions claim that gays are looking for "special rights" because our rights are already protected by the U.S. Constitution. This is legally incorrect. Only eight states (to date, 7/1/94) and just over 100 municipalities have non-discrimination policies that include sexual orientation; in every other place, gay workers live and work in fear. Without some guarantee from their employer, at the very minimum, they have no reason to feel secure in their jobs, and, in some cases, their homes.

Neither the U.S. Constitution, the Civil Rights Acts of 1964 and 1972, the Pregnancy Discrimination Act of 1978, the Age Discrimination Act of 1978, nor the Americans with Disabilities Act of 1990 extend their protections to sexual orientation. In fact, many gays argue that it is not they who are looking for "special rights," but rather it is heterosexuals who already have all the special rights–the right to legal validation of their relationships, the right to inherit property, the right to establish joint accounts and mortgages, the right of next-of-kin status, the right of visitation, and the right of access to records, to name a few.

If a company has a policy of non-discrimination that is not inclusive of sexual orientation, then the first step is to have that classification added. And if a company already has such an inclusive policy, then it owes it to all of its employees to back it up in the form of equitable benefits plans. A 1993 study released by the National Gay and Lesbian Task Force (1993) found that just over five percent of the Fortune 1000 companies that responded have benefits for gay and lesbian people; but over 70% of those same companies have inclusive non-discrimination policies in place. These numbers need to be brought into better balance.

Management and Consultants

The next step in the implementation of domestic partner benefits is to win upper management's approval of the concept and then of the actual plan. Getting these people on board is the only way to ensure success of the proposal. Whether it is one highly interested senior management representative or an entire task-force, their support will be contingent on being provided with two basic sets of information: how much is this going to cost? and exactly why should we do this? Thus any party broaching this idea should present their justifications with arguments and data about those two things at the very beginning of the document or presentation.

All arguments made must be based in fact and not on emotion. The concept of "fairness" is an appropriate subtle theme, but arguments related to profitability, competitive and market advantages, and productivity will get the proposal much farther. The presenter(s) must be up to date on all cost figures, statistics, and relevant equations. Senior management will not seriously consider any proposal that leaves them with a lot of action items; you must leave them with only decision points.

It is at this juncture that many organizations will find it more efficient and effective to turn to a consultant: efficient because a consultant specializing in domestic partner benefits will have all pertinent information at hand and can therefore save management a lot of time, and effective because use of a consultant removes emotion from the equation.

Any time an organization is considering a progressive step, like the implementation of domestic partner benefits, it is making a significant statement about the organization as a whole. The decision, whether to implement benefits, will have ramifications for the enterprise both internally and externally. Internally, the organization is sending a clear message to all its personnel about how it views equitable treatment, and externally, the organization is making a statement to society as a whole about its values and how it intends to conduct itself within the bigger picture.

Consider Apple Corporation and the difficulties it faced in Williamson, Texas in late 1993. Plans to put a very large manufacturing facility with the potential to employ over 20,000 workers came to a halt when the Town Council voted to refuse Apple a standard tax-abatement on the facility because Apple extends domestic partner benefits to the partners of its gay employees. It was only after the Governor of the State (Ann Richards) interceded that Apple ultimately decided to establish a much smaller customer service facility in Williamson. And they did get the tax abatement for it.

Apple's experience of having to stand behind its principles is not an uncommon one. The Bank of America succumbed to pressure from the Boy Scouts of America to drop any talk of domestic partner benefits, AT&T is facing pressure from the so-called "religious right" over its courting of the gay market, and VISA is also under fire for having vocally and financially supported 1994's Gay Games in New York City. These are but a few examples. Therefore, when a company decides to uphold its non-discrimination policy inclusive of orientation, it must have a firm understanding of what the risks are, who their adversaries are, and most importantly, who their allies are. A consultant cannot only explain the ins and outs of the benefits themselves, but can offer vital information about strategies that other companies have used to successfully implement them. A competent consultant also represents a gateway to the literally hundreds of organizations that stand ready to support the enterprise's course of action.

Whether a consultant is utilized or a task-force of concerned personnel and management comes together to influence policy, the very first step is to make sure that the company's non-discrimination policy expressly includes sexual orientation. That is the foundation upon which any rational argument for the implementation of the benefits—in whatever form—must be built. Benefits, the way we are compensated and how we provide for our families as we each define them, is an intrinsically emotional issue. But it is important that emotion not be part of the argument because benefits and compensation are, in reality, strictly business decisions.

People will argue that it is easier to win these benefits in the "more liberal" areas of the U.S., such as the Northeast and the West Coast, and it is undeniable that most of the companies that have these types of programs are in those places. But it is equally undeniable that American Micro Devices in Austin, Texas, awarded these benefits to its employees in the same week that the City of Austin itself repealed its own domestic partner benefits plan (this reversal is under appeal) due to pressure from "the conservative right." It is also undeniable that the University of Minnesota and the City of Minneapolis were and are leaders in the fight for equal treatment, and that the State of Wisconsin enforces some of the most equitable statutes, including those that protect on the basis of sexual orientation, in the U.S. The point is, if people stick to facts and logic and utilize the appropriate information, they stand an excellent chance of winning the benefits regardless of their geographic location.

Any single employee can be the impetus to start this ball rolling. At Banyan Systems in Massachusetts, it was the action of one and then two employees that won the benefits. At Lotus, three employees carried the banner. Any single employee can reach out to others in order to establish a task-force, or can approach the human resources department and ask them to help. The amount of personal involvement is a matter of individual preference. It is true that a certain amount of courage is involved, but persistence and reaching out to resources both within and outside of the company are the real keys to success.

For instance, when we make a presentation to potential implementers of these benefits, the first part of the program is spent talking about the difficult social and emotional issues surrounding the question. We explain the nature of homosexuality, delve into the myths, and give people the opportunity to express their thoughts, fears, and ideas on the subject. In other words, we try to get everyone in the room on the same page. That page is the one that covers why gays are entitled to and want these types of benefits from their employer, and why their requirements are valid. Once everyone has agreed, or at least is willing to consider, that gay/lesbian employees have legitimate concerns that can positively or negatively affect the bottom line performance of the company, then we can proceed with a discussion of the benefits themselves.

Relevant management should be presented with information, facts and figures that address the proposed benefits, including (in the following order):

1. a definition of domestic partner benefits,
2. a justification for the implementation of the benefits in the organization,
3. the meaning of a non-discrimination policy that expressly includes sexual orientation,
4. requirements for qualification as a domestic partner,
5. recommendation of which benefits currently offered to legal spouses/dependents would be extended to partners and/or their dependents,
6. examples of the projected cost of the benefits to the company,
7. examples of the projected cost of the benefits to the employees who elect them,
8. an explanation and example of the tax ramifications to all parties,
9. an explanation as to the ways the implementation of these benefits would affect the enterprise,
10. information as to the position of the insurance industry in general, and insurers in particular, in regard to these benefits,

11. a detailed plan to handle registration for and administration of these benefits, and
12. a detailed plan for the communication of the benefit plan to all employees and to the outside world.

It would be naive of us not to acknowledge that sometimes all the comprehensive presentations in the world will not be enough to combat homophobia if that turns out to be at the crux of why an organization chooses not to implement these benefits. The only way to combat homophobia is through education. If benefits are refused for reasons that can be traced to ignorance about sexual orientation, then the group of individuals potentially affected by the proposal, with the aid of helping social service professionals, will find it necessary to engage in educational efforts to counter this ignorance.

Employees and Coworkers

Once agreed upon, and while all the final logistical arrangements are being made, a great deal of attention is necessary to determine how the plan will be communicated to employees and, in fact, to the world. There may be resistance to these benefits, especially if the enterprise chooses to offer them to gay couples only. Straight, un-married-but-no-less-committed couples are going to have a hard time with that. Generally, companies that have implemented partner benefits to gay-only couples have done so with the thinking that since gays cannot legally marry, they are simply trying to make things equitable. Those who have decided to offer these benefits to straight, unmarried couples as well, have done so because they believe that if their policy is not to discriminate on the basis of orientation, then they cannot discriminate against heterosexuals who choose, for whatever reason, not to marry. Regardless of a company's decision on this matter, be prepared to provide some level of education to the entire employee base that covers not only the benefits themselves, but all the underlying issues behind the benefits' implementation.

The importance of company-wide education at this juncture cannot be overemphasized. So many of the objections to the implementation of domestic partner benefits that recognize the validity of same-sex relationships (and to a lesser degree, opposite-sex relationships that exist without benefit of legal marriage) are based upon ignorance about those relationships and about gay people in general.

Every company considering benefits should also consider the extent to which its employee education programs cover these difficult and sensitive subjects. In developing written or verbal communication plans about any new benefits, the extent to which the general employee population has been informed about the nature and reason for the changes must be considered.

If a company does not offer diversity training of any kind, it should implement it. If its diversity training has steered away from issues related to sexual orientation and AIDS education because of the difficulties inherent in those subjects, it must find the courage to include them. It is difficult, if not impossible, to effectively communicate with parties who are ignorant of the facts.

Companies should provide straightforward and simple documentation about the plan. Many companies experience great success in introducing these benefits in conjunction with the overhaul or retooling of all of their benefits packages, thereby creating a need for everyone in the organization to reenlist or reevaluate their choices at the same time. This gives the company the opportunity to position and explain the domestic partner benefits as just one more option in a well thought out and constructed benefits plan. Wherever possible, it is appropriate to hold a meeting or series of meetings to have the benefits explained by the appropriate personnel rather than just by memo. Representatives from senior management should be present at each meeting, thereby lending their visible support to all the programs. Senior management sets the tone from the very beginning through the very end. Their involvement is crucial to the success of the endeavor.

Finally, implementors of the policy must make sure that there is a streamlined, efficient, and accessible mechanism in place for people to ask questions, voice comments, and discuss concerns (anonymously if necessary). This includes human resources personnel managers and social service providers who should be given adequate information and training to discuss, answer and address employee questions and concerns.

CONCLUSION

Unless companies make provisions for the new workplace diversity, be it gay, straight, or otherwise, individual and organizational performance will suffer. Gay people are beginning to understand and utilize the fact that if they can win the battles over issues like non-discrimination policies that are expressly inclusive of orientation, and benefits in the workplace that reflect the realities of their families, that those victories will eventually spread to society as a whole. At that point, the laws and the ways in which the various bounties of society are distributed will begin to reflect reality, and not homophobic or heterosexist principles.

REFERENCES

American Civil Liberties Union. (1992). *Legislative briefing series: Domestic partner benefits.* New York: ACLU.

Apple Corporation. (1992). Study of the implementation of domestic partner benefits. Internal report, Sunnyvale, CA.

Columbia University. (1993). Columbia University Domestic Partner Policy for Health Care Benefits. New York: Columbia University.

Conahan, F. (1992). Department of Defense policy on homosexuality. Washington, DC: United States General Accounting Office.

Cox, T. (1993). *Cultural diversity in organizations: Theory, research & practice.* San Francisco: Berrett-Koehler.

Davis, L. (1985). Group work practice with ethnic minorities of color. In M. Sundel (Ed.), *Individual change through small groups* (pp. 324-343). New York: Free Press.

Mass Mutual Life Insurance Company. (1989). *American families value study.* Internal report, Boston, MA.

McNaught, B. (1993). *Gay issues in the workplace.* New York: St. Martin's Press.

National Gay and Lesbian Task Force. (1993). *Workplace policy study.* New York: NGLTF.

National Leadership Coalition on AIDS. (1993). *HIV/AIDS: A guide for employers and managers.* Washington, DC: National Leadership Coalition on AIDS.

Newsweek. (1994). Homophobia, February 14, 42-45.

Rovira v. AT&T. (1991). 760 F SUPP 376 Southern District New York.

Sherman, A. (1993). Domestic partner benefits. *Executive letter.* Boston: The Segal Company.

Time. (1994). Pride and prejudice: Bumping up against the limits of tolerance, June 27, 55-59.

United States Bureau of the Census. (1994). *Marriage and family division report on the family.* Washington, DC: U.S. Government Printing Office.

University of Iowa. (1991). Domestic partner coverage. *Report to the Chancellor.* Ames, IA: University of Iowa.

Van Sluys, L. (1991). *A research paper on domestic partner benefits.* Lincolnshire, IL: Hewitt Associates.

Winfeld, L., & Spielman, S. (1995). *Out in the open: Gay people in the workplace.* New York: American Management Association Communications.

Woods, J.D. (1993). *The corporate closet: The professional lives of gay men in America.* New York: Free Press.

The Impact of Gay, Lesbian, and Bisexual Workplace Issues on Productivity

Bob Powers

SUMMARY. People in organizations lack the skills, knowledge, tools, and resources to effectively address gay, lesbian, bisexual, and transgender workplace issues. Consequently, most organizations fail to attain optimum performance from the approximately ten percent of their population who are sexual minorities. Two examples of what occurs when these issues are not addressed are: (1) gays, lesbians, bisexuals and transgendered employees do not feel included in the organization. When people, any people, are excluded rather than included it is almost impossible to expect optimal performance; and, (2) organizations send messages to gay, lesbian, bisexual and transgendered employees that encourage them to hide their sexual orientation at work. When employees devote energy to hiding–as gays, lesbians, bisexual and transgendered employees often do to protect themselves and their livelihood–performance suffers. In this article, these workplace issues are brought out of the corporate closet and into the mainstream of business performance. *[Article copies available from The Haworth Document Delivery Service: 1-800-342-9678.]*

People in organizations often lack the knowledge, skills, tools, and resources to effectively address gay, lesbian and bisexual workplace issues. Consequently, most organizations fail to attain opti-

Bob Powers, MS, is President of Bob Powers and Associates, 3651 21st Street, San Francisco, CA 94114.

[Haworth co-indexing entry note]: "The Impact of Gay, Lesbian, and Bisexual Workplace Issues on Productivity." Powers, Bob. Co-published simultaneously in *Journal of Gay & Lesbian Social Services* (The Haworth Press, Inc.) Vol. 4, No. 4, 1996, pp. 79-90; and: *Sexual Identity on the Job: Issues and Services* (ed: Alan L. Ellis, and Ellen D. B. Riggle) The Haworth Press, Inc., 1996, pp. 79-90; and: *Sexual Identity on the Job: Issues and Services* (ed: Alan L. Ellis, and Ellen D. B. Riggle) Harrington Park Press, an imprint of The Haworth Press, Inc., 1996, pp. 79-90. Single or multiple copies of this article are available from The Haworth Document Delivery Service [1-800-342-9678, 9:00 a.m. - 5:00 p.m. (EST)].

© 1996 by The Haworth Press, Inc. All rights reserved.

mum performance from the ten percent of their population who are sexual minorities.

When people lack knowledge, skills, tools and/or resources they tend to operate in dysfunctional ways. Sexual orientation workplace issues have been ignored or inadequately addressed in most organizations. This has resulted in sexual minorities feeling *excluded* from their own organizations. When people, any people, feel excluded rather than included it is almost impossible to perform optimally. In addition, organizations send messages to gay, lesbian, and bisexual employees that encourage them to hide their sexual orientation at work. When employees devote energy to hiding–as gays, lesbians, and bisexuals often do to protect themselves and their livelihood–performance suffers. The homophobia that exists in our nation also contributes to societal problems, such as the high levels of teen suicide and teen runaways among gay, lesbian and bisexual youth, and of course, AIDS, to name a few. These problems spill over into the workplace and adversely affect performance.

In this article, I will consider issues surrounding inclusion in the workplace, then explore the messages managers send to employees regarding sexual orientation and the hiding that takes place as a result of these messages. I will also look at societal issues and problems related to sexual orientation and examine the impact of each of these on performance. Finally, I will describe how managers and employees and those who consult with each of these groups can develop the knowledge, skills, tools and resources to manage these workplace issues effectively and optimize performance.

INCLUSION IN THE WORKPLACE

In the late 1970s I was moved from Pacific Telephone, where I was head of an internal consulting and performance analysis organization, to AT&T headquarters in New Jersey. I had been brought to headquarters on a promotion to manage the corporation's Training and Development Organization. While I was "out" to friends and family, I had not yet come out at work, except to a handful of other gays and lesbians in the corporation. As a gay man, I did not feel included or welcomed. There were no visible role models (other successful openly gay men or women) and no one publicly addressed these issues. In fact, the words gay and lesbian were generally not spoken in the workplace (or in society), except quietly by gays and lesbians or derisively by heterosexuals. Most people still considered homosexuality a sickness. Only a year or two had passed since the American Psychological Association had removed homosexuality from its list of mental illnesses. So, the workplace, reflective of society at large, did not open its arms to anyone whose sexual orientation differed from heterosexuality.

Excluding people forces them to expend their energies on non-work related items, such as finding ways to network, and supporting and protecting themselves from abuse and discrimination. Exclusion leaves people feeling isolated and uses up energies that could otherwise be devoted to being productive at work. And exclusion is costly. Many organizations have paid large amounts of money as a result of lawsuits filed because women, the disabled, racial minorities and others have been excluded. One such example of this can be seen in the massive amounts of taxpayer money that have been used to keep gays and lesbians out of the military. Organizations simply have not learned the lesson that exclusion affects productivity and the bottom line.

The corporate world's current attention to diversity seems to imply inclusion. Yet in America, diversity is more often exclusive than inclusive. Most corporate diversity policies *do not* include gays, lesbians, bisexuals, or transgender people. While the number of organizations that *do* include these groups is growing, most organizations exclude them, and some even deny their existence.

I believe that organizations that exclude *any* group from their diversity policies and practices do a huge disservice to the credibility of their entire diversity program, because when one group sees another group excluded, they know that they could be the next group excluded. Whenever a group of people is excluded the message organizations send to all groups is that their commitment to diversity may be little more than lip service. When employees see organizations giving lip service to diversity, or any other program, any integrity these programs might have had is diminished. And lip service *is* expensive. Corporations are expending millions of dollars annually on diversity programs. Yet, the productivity gains that can come from people feeling included, rather than excluded, are not realized.

Ask yourself, how inclined would you be to go out of your way to ensure an organization's success when that organization excludes you, *for any reason*. When people are excluded or not welcomed into the fold of a group, optimal performance does not take place.

In addition, if people are ignored, as gays and lesbians have been for decades, they tend to do one of two things. They wither away or they act up. For much of the current century gays and lesbians have withered away in their corporate closets. Today, as evidenced by the massive turnouts for both the 1993 March on Washington and the 1994 Stonewall March, the numbers of Americans stepping proudly out of the closet have skyrocketed. Numerous corporations now have gay employee organizations and many others offer traditional benefits to same sex couples. In addition, companies like IKEA and AT&T are marketing directly to their gay and lesbian customers. And mass media has finally taken notice of the explosion of gay pride and activism. The attention paid to issues related to sexual orientation, like "Gays in the Military," the 1993 March on Washington, and the statewide anti-gay initiatives in Colorado and Oregon, has increased Americans' awareness of these issues. No longer content to wither away, today's sexual minorities are acting up.

Organizations that exclude gays, lesbians, bisexuals and other sexual minorities are losing the energy, resourcefulness and creativity that these groups of people possess. Instead of putting these quality traits into improving workplace performance, sexual minorities are forced to expend their energies to survive, to protect themselves, as well as to flourish as well as they can in a homophobic environment. This is energy, resourcefulness and creativity that could be put to use in improving America's productivity and bottom line.

HIDING IN THE WORKPLACE

For decades American business has sent messages to employees that it's not okay to be gay. Sometimes, these messages are (thought to be) subtle, like "It's okay to be gay as long as you keep it quiet/don't flaunt it/don't try to impose it on me or anyone else in the company." Sometimes they are blatant, like "We don't want any of your kind in our organizations!" or "There has never been a homosexual working here and there never will be!" Regardless of the subtlety, the message is basically the same: homosexuals must hide to survive. For many, hiding became a necessity. Those, like Lisa, who stepped out risked losing their jobs. Until Lisa came out as a lesbian, she had been considered a top-notch performer in her firm. All of the following examples are excerpts taken from interviews/reports in Powers and Ellis (1995).

> Soon (after I came out), I was hounded by my immediate supervisor. Ron ripped apart everything I wrote, claiming this fact was misrepresented, that sentence was awkward, this comma was misplaced. He'd harangue in this way for two to three hours each morning. In the afternoon, I would implement his changes. The next morning he would browbeat me again, contradicting much of what he'd told me the day before. Eventually, I was summoned into the president's office. He asked, "How do you like working here?" "Fine, I like it just fine," I responded. He sighed and looked at his desk top. Eventually he said, "Things just aren't working out." Again, he sighed and we waited. Finally, he said, "I don't think you'll be working here any more." I asked if he was saying I was fired. He said, "I guess you could say that."

Over the years, to protect their livelihood and sometimes their lives, sexual minorities stayed hidden in their corporate closets. To survive homophobia, they often formed gay and lesbian underground organizations or networks.

> I met Robert in the mid-seventies. He introduced me to the gay underground at work. This was a network of lesbians and gay men, who communicated with one another about corporate policies, people and events in an effort to survive a homophobic environment. All of us hid our sexual orientation, from everyone but each other.

The energy it takes to "hide" is immense. Keeping things inside and responding to the simplest question takes great concentration. For example, when I met the man I came to love, I was bursting to tell my co-workers about it. Yet, my fear kept me from even revealing that I was seeing someone. I would respond to a simple question like, "What did you do over the weekend?" with a pitiful, "Oh, I just spent it with some friends." I constantly cut off any genuine communication. Everything I said and did had to cover up my sexual orientation, which took tremendous energy. Once I came out at work, I was able to tell people what I did and who I loved without putting all that effort into hiding. The freedom I felt was exhilarating. I blossomed, and so did my creativity and my productivity. After all, I could now expend that energy on work, rather than on hiding.

Hiding also takes a toll on one's self-esteem. Joe, a Human Resource Professional, describes his evening at the home of the president of his company.

> During dinner, the president's wife asked me if I was married. I told her I wasn't legally married. She nodded her understanding and went on to tell me how, despite her husband's protest, her son had lived with a woman for a period of time, but it was alright now because they had married. She then asked my girlfriend's name. I got very embarrassed and tried to change the subject. She persisted and asked why I wouldn't tell her the name of my girlfriend. By now, we had attracted the attention of the other dinner guests. I was mortified and asked her to stop asking. She ended the conversation by winking and saying that she understood. I have no idea if she really understood. I do know that I felt angry and ashamed that I didn't have the courage to talk about Thaddeus as the other employees at the dinner spoke of their spouses. While I excused myself by acknowledging that I simply didn't feel safe sharing about my life with the company's first lady, I resolved that I would never suppress myself in a similar situation.

Joe's experience is not uncommon. When people hide, they are vulnerable to being "found out," forced into telling lies and/or enmeshed in isolation. Joe's resolve did lead to his coming out at work. Now his focus goes into being creative, productive and resourceful, rather than hiding and dealing with the worry and stress that comes with the possibility of being found out.

I recently spoke to sixty or so managers, most of whom are heterosexual, on the impact of hiding in the workplace. I asked for a volunteer (a heterosexual parent) to participate in a role play. A young father of two agreed to participate. His task was simple. He was told that he was going to join a corporation where being a heterosexual was tantamount to losing one's job. The sixty or so participants, I advised, would be on the lookout for any signs that he might be a heterosexual. So, I suggested to the participant that he "cover up" his heterosexuality at all costs. I then painted the following scenario: It is Monday morning and we are both "on break."

I began by asking, "What did you do over the weekend?"

"Oh, I went to the beach," he replied.

"Oh, who did you go with?" I inquired.

"Oh, just some people I know," he said.

That was a rather odd response, I thought (so did the sixty or so observers), so I asked, "What beach did you go to?"

He named a beach in Marin County.

"Isn't that a family beach?" I asked somewhat derogatorily.

"Oh . . . (stumbling as he spoke) it . . . it . . . has all kinds of people," he replied.

"Really?" I stated and asked, "What kinds are those?"

It did not take more than thirty seconds for this father of two to give off signals of his heterosexuality. When we debriefed the role play, participants were struck by how easy it is to signal one's heterosexuality and awed by how difficult it is to hide it. The only road open for this father of two was to lie, evade, omit, and isolate, all of which consumes energy and creates stress.

And it really does not matter who is hiding or what is being hidden–most people have tried to hide one thing or another. The fact is when people are forced into hiding, productivity suffers.

HOMOPHOBIA IN SOCIETY AND ITS IMPACT ON PRODUCTIVITY

Larry watched his lover of almost twenty years die of AIDS. Because homophobia was rampant in his workplace, he had remained closeted throughout his almost twenty-year career with the firm.

I was forced to go through my grief alone because I was unable to tell my coworkers that the most important person in my life had died. I eventually suffered a breakdown of spirit and work.

Alan quit his job at the end of one year.

My managers believed that I quit because I had not been challenged by the work. That thought never even entered my mind. I left because I was simply too absorbed by the conflict between my sexual identity and my religious beliefs to focus on my work.

Regardless of the issue—AIDS, teen suicide, gays in the military—the homophobia which exists in our nation creates problems which spill over into and affect the workplace. I think most people would agree that having a child run away from home or commit suicide would affect a person's performance. So, what do teen runaway and teen suicide statistics have to do with sexual orientation and the workplace? It has been estimated that thirty percent of all teen runaways are homosexual and over thirty percent of teen suicides are committed by gay and lesbian youth. Homophobia, a lack of knowledge and a lack of skills and comfort, keep family members from addressing sexual orientation issues with their children. As a result, gay kids stay hidden, isolated in fear and self-loathing. Steeped in ignorance, many are ill-equipped to handle the homophobia that exists within their families and within society. Often, they run away or take their own lives. No parents can work productively when such crises enter their lives. And heterosexual parents find themselves in a closet similar to that of Larry when they fear letting others know they have a gay child or relative, not to mention a related tragedy to handle.

There is a long list of societal issues—AIDS, bereavement leave, teen runaways, teen suicides, gays in the military, religious teachings, and so forth—that affect workplace performance. As long as we remain ignorant about these issues, we are destined to fall short of our workplace potential.

Ignorance may be bliss is some settings, but in the corporate world, ignorance, or a lack of knowledge, is one of the prime reasons organizations fail. *Fortune Magazine,* in its December, 1991 cover story entitled, "Gay in Corporate America," said that even most educated people are misinformed about gay and lesbian issues. So, organizations that lack knowledge about gay, lesbian and bisexual employees and customers, are at a serious competitive disadvantage. And the competition is coming out of the corporate closet!

America's top corporations, from Apple to Xerox, are beginning to recognize and address this large base of employees and customers. Approximately one-half of Fortune 1000 companies now offer some workplace protection to their gay and lesbian employees and many others offer spouse and other benefits, as well. And why not? Gay, lesbian and bisexual employees make up anywhere from four to ten percent of the workforce. Even higher percentages exist in some industries. And the gay, lesbian and bisexual customer base is estimated by marketing firms at 25 million people, with a purchasing power of $394 billion, a median household annual income of $42,000 for men and $39,000 for women, with an average age of 39.3 years (Powers & Ellis, 1995). With numbers such as these, and the opportunities they present, why has it taken so long for American firms to wake up to this profitable market? The answers are obvious.

The issue of sexuality (in general), and variations from heterosexuality (in particular), is controversial and steeped in ignorance. Like most people, managers tend to avoid controversy and ignore situations where they feel unable to manage the outcomes. Because gay, lesbian and bisexual employees and customers lived quiet, even closeted corporate lives they were invisible, perpetuating the myth that "they don't exist in our company." Today, most corporations recognize that sexual minorities do exist and that they no longer are content in remaining closeted or even quiet.

> . . . down in the trenches at many companies, unfamiliar lifestyles are being demystified at lunch, over coffee and in meetings. Mere familiarity begins to change perceptions. Until recently, most Americans couldn't say the words 'gay' and 'lesbian' without thinking that something weird was coming out of their mouths.
>
> *New York Times* (1993)

SEXUAL ORIENTATION
AND WORKPLACE PERFORMANCE

I have spent most of the past twenty-five years devoted to improving the way human beings perform in the workplace. This work has led me to develop two premises about people and performance.

One, if people *do not* have to hide *and* if they feel included, they will perform better than if they must hide and feel excluded. Two, people lack the knowledge, skills, tools and resources to successfully manage sexual orientation workplace issues. A lack of knowledge, skills, tools and resources are four of the primary reasons why people fail to perform as desired (Rossett, 1992; Powers, 1992).

To gain knowledge, managers must begin to learn about the lives of gay, lesbian, bisexual *and* heterosexual employees, bosses, co-workers and customers who have come to terms with sexual orientation workplace issues and learn about the issues within society that affect workplace performance. A good way to start is to ask an openly gay person, "Would you please tell me what it's like to be gay in this company?"

> In 1992, I had my first real association with an openly gay man. He was a person on my staff. I didn't know him well, but when I heard he told his work group that he was gay, I decided to talk to him. I told him that I thought he was a brave man and I wanted him to know that I would be there to support him if he needed me. I knew it would be difficult for him. I guess because I felt different from most people around me, I could understand what he might be going through.

That decision set Constance, a heterosexual African-American corporate trainer, on a path to learn about homosexuality even though her religious upbringing referred to homosexuality as a sin. Constance believes the knowledge she has gained has made her a better manager.

And most managers need to be better in addressing these issues. Managers need to develop skills that enable them to select diversity-sensitive employees, to define employee responsibility (see the following) and set performance expectations relative to these issues. In addition, managers need to learn how to provide feedback, recognition and rewards to employees to reinforce and strengthen their performance in these areas.

Employee Responsibility

It is the employee's responsibility regarding sexual orientation to: (1) promote acceptance of ALL (gays, lesbians and bisexuals included) within the organization by aggressively supporting the company's diversity policies; and, (2) ensure that NO ONE (gays, lesbians and bisexuals included) is discriminated against for any reason, whatsoever.

Powers and Ellis (1995) identify 101 ways to make the workplace more inclusive, including the following:

- When interviewing candidates for jobs, let them know that your organization is all-inclusive.
- Encourage lesbian and gay employees to point out training and business policies and practices that discriminate based upon the sexual orientation of employees and customers.
- Especially welcome same sex partners at company events.
- Respond to homophobic jokes and statements, by saying, "That's not okay in this organization."
- Route business and news articles about gay and lesbian workplace issues to people within your organization.
- Let your gay, lesbian and bisexual employees know that you will stand up for them in the event they experience any discrimination.
- DO NOT assume that employees (or customers) are heterosexual.
- Respond to criticism by referring to your desire to create and be part of an all-inclusive workplace.
- Smile when you say the words "gay," "lesbian," and "bisexual."

Having adequate tools and resources is an essential component of maintaining top-notch performance. There is a comprehensive list of community organizations within the United States and Canada offering related services such as speakers bureaus and outreach programs. Computer bulletin boards also provide access to information regarding major news articles, books, and academic research articles addressing gay, lesbian, and bisexual issues in the workplace.

Now that the veil of silence that has kept these issues so closeted for so many years has been lifted, businesses across the nation are beginning to look at these issues with a new eye. One by one, corporations are moving out of their denial surrounding gays in the workplace. As they do, they begin to gain knowledge and skill and identify tools and resources that will forever change the way they manage their gay, lesbian and bisexual employees and customers, as well as affect the bottom line. And the bottom line is that productivity will be increased when people do not have to use their energy and resources to hide and protect. The bottom line will be increased when people feel included rather than excluded. And the bottom line will be increased when employees devote their time to handling business rather than handling the overwhelming effects caused by homophobia in society at large and in the workplace in particular.

REFERENCES

Fortune Magazine. (1991). Gay in corporate America, December.

New York Times. (1993). A quiet liberation for gay and lesbian employees, June 14.

Powers, B. (1992). Strategic alignment. In H.D. Stolovitch & E.J. Keeps (Eds.), *Handbook of human performance technology* (pp. 247-258). San Francisco: Jossey Bass.

Powers, B., & Ellis, A.L. (1995). *A manager's guide to sexual orientation in the workplace.* New York: Routledge.

Rossett, A. (1992). Analysis of human performance problems. In H.D. Stolovitch & E.J. Keeps (Eds.), *Handbook of human performance technology* (pp. 97-113). San Francisco: Jossey Bass.

Gay and Lesbian Career Counseling: Special Career Counseling Issues

Mark Pope

SUMMARY. This article reviews the special issues for gay men and lesbian women which have been identified in the career counseling and development literature. The special issues include collecting special career information for use with gay and lesbian clients, coping with counselor bias, educating self and others about the special developmental issues of lesbians and gays, "coming out" in the workplace and career, handling issues of discrimination, being aware of occupational role models and networking, testing and counseling, transitioning from school to work, dealing with couples and other family issues, and advocating for gay and lesbian clients and their rights within the majority culture. Specific practices are identified in conjunction with each issue. *[Article copies available from The Haworth Document Delivery Service: 1-800-342-9678.]*

Although many mental health professionals already have gay and lesbian clients who are seeking career development assistance, many of these mental health professionals are providing career services without knowledge of the special career development needs of gay and lesbian clients. The purpose of this article is to outline some of the special issues which have been reported in the

Mark Pope, EdD, is President of Career Decisions, a career counseling and consulting firm, 760 Market Street, Suite 962, San Francisco, CA 94102-2304.

[Haworth co-indexing entry note]: "Gay and Lesbian Career Counseling: Special Career Counseling Issues." Pope, Mark. Co-published simultaneously in *Journal of Gay & Lesbian Social Services* (The Haworth Press, Inc.) Vol. 4, No. 4, 1996, pp. 91-105; and: *Sexual Identity on the Job: Issues and Services* (ed: Alan L. Ellis, and Ellen D. B. Riggle) The Haworth Press, Inc., 1996, pp. 91-105; and: *Sexual Identity on the Job: Issues and Services* (ed: Alan L. Ellis, and Ellen D. B. Riggle) Harrington Park Press, an imprint of The Haworth Press, Inc., 1996, pp. 91-105. Single or multiple copies of this article are available from The Haworth Document Delivery Service [1-800-342-9678, 9:00 a.m. - 5:00 p.m. (EST)].

© 1996 by The Haworth Press, Inc. All rights reserved.

literature and to identify some of the specific practices which are suggested.

RESEARCH ON GAY AND LESBIAN
CAREER DEVELOPMENT

Weinberg and Bell (1971), in the most comprehensive compendium of research on homosexuality published at the time, presented an annotated bibliography on homosexuality. They noted even then that "... the focus of these researchers and commentators all too often has precluded any reference to those processes–both sociological and psychological–which maintain the homosexual's career" (p. xii).

Several published works on gay and lesbian mental health issues have included a "mention" of career development and career counseling as important aspects of gay and lesbian mental health. In these articles, the issues associated with lesbian and gay career development are generally addressed as a subcomponent of an overall treatment of counseling psychology methods with gay and lesbian clients (Buhrke, 1989; Buhrke, Ben-Ezra, Hurley, & Ruprecht, 1992; Buhrke & Douce, 1991; Gelso & Fassinger, 1990; Fassinger, 1994; Gonsiorek, 1984; Shannon & Wood, 1991).

The decade of the 1990s has seen an explosion, relative to previous decades, of published materials in gay and lesbian career development. In only four years (1990-1993), 19 articles have been published and, as a result, the literature in this area has more than doubled (a total of thirty-one articles have been published on this topic). This work has come about as authors/researchers, conference and convention program chairs, editors of professional journals, and publishing companies have decided it was time to bring this research "out of the closet" and into the mainstream.

Elliott (1990) presented a paper at the American Psychological Association Annual Convention in Boston sponsored by Division 17 (Counseling Psychology) that outlined career development concerns for gays and lesbians, and he followed with an article in the *Career Development Quarterly*. Pope and his associates have presented papers at regional and national conferences (Pope, 1991; Pope, 1993; Pope & Jelly, 1991; Pope, Rodriguez, & Chang, 1992;

Pope & Schecter, 1992) and the American Counseling Association published a book of case studies on lesbian and gay issues (Dworkin & Gutierrez, 1992) which included chapters oriented to career development (Orzek, 1992) and career testing issues (Pope, 1992). Diamant (1993) edited a book on gay and lesbian issues in the workplace with important chapters on hiring, firing, promotion, the military, the church, helping professions, educators, the prisons, athletics, older gays, "coming out" in the workplace, stress, and AIDS. Special issues or sections of major professional journals have been devoted to lesbian and gay issues in counseling, including career development issues. The *Career Development Quarterly*, the flagship journal of the National Career Development Association, published a section on gay and lesbian career development (including Belz, 1993; Croteau & Hedstrom, 1993; Elliott, 1993).

These activities led to a presentation by a panel of researchers at the January, 1994 National Career Development Association Conference in Albuquerque, New Mexico. The title of the presentation was "Gay and Lesbian Career Development: Setting a Research Agenda." Panelists included Jeffrey P. Prince, Director of the Career Counseling Program at the University of California-Berkeley; Ruth E. Fassinger, Professor of Counseling Psychology at the University of Maryland-College Park; Y. Barry Chung, doctoral student in Counseling Psychology at the University of Illinois-Champaign; and Mark Pope, President of Career Decisions, a San Francisco career counseling and consulting firm, and a member of the faculty at Stanford University, San Francisco State University, University of San Francisco, and Golden Gate University. Panelists reviewed the literature in gay and lesbian career development and presented their findings. Prince (1994) discussed issues of gay male identity formation and career development; Fassinger (1994) reviewed the extensive literature on lesbian identity formation and career development; Chung (1994) reported on the literature on gay and lesbian career choice; and Pope (1994) presented the findings of his review of the literature on career counseling interventions with gay males and lesbians.

CAREER COUNSELING ISSUES

There are specific issues which are reported in the literature as being important for gays and lesbians. These issues include collecting special career information for use with gay and lesbian clients, coping with counselor bias, educating self and others about the special developmental issues of lesbians and gays, "coming out" in the workplace and career, handling issues of discrimination, being aware of occupational role models and networking, testing and counseling, transitioning from school to work, dealing with couples and other family issues, and advocating for gay and lesbian clients and their rights within the majority culture.

Special Career Information

Career counselors who work with lesbians and gay men have very little quality data to use in helping their clients. Brown (1975) identified the types of questions which the lesbian or gay client might need answers to: Is a large university or a small liberal arts college more accepting of homosexuality? Is a religious or a public college a better choice? Are some jobs closed to the "out" gay or lesbian? What industries are most discriminatory? Is being gay ever an advantage in one's career? Is a person's sexual orientation an important question when making career decisions? (pp. 234-235).

Counselor Bias

Counselors are admonished to examine their own biases. This is important for issues of both ethics and effectiveness (Belz, 1993; Brown, 1975; Chung & Harmon, in press; Hetherington, Hiller-brand, & Etringer, 1989; Hetherington & Orzek, 1989; Morgan & Brown, 1991; Pope, 1992). Issues here include referring the client to someone else if the counselor is not gay/lesbian affirmative (Belz, 1993; Brown, 1975; Croteau & Hedstrom, 1993), learning the model of lesbian/gay identity development (Morgan & Brown, 1991), being familiar with gay/lesbian culture (Pope, 1991), and accepting the client's own frame of reference (Orzek, 1992).

Special Developmental Issues

Cass (1979) identified the developmental stages which gays and lesbians must accomplish: (1) identity confusion, (2) identity comparison, (3) identity tolerance, (4) identity acceptance, (5) identity pride, and (6) identity synthesis. These stages are part of what is widely termed the "coming out" process.

Morgan and Brown (1991), in reanalyzing data from two previously-gathered, large, lesbian samples, specifically addressed how the lesbian career development process seemed to fit into previously published minority group models of career development and how it is also unique. Using Cass's (1979) model of gay and lesbian identity development, they identified the process of identity development as one of the most important life processes for lesbian women. They noted that the age that the individual lesbian goes through the identity development stage is important. For example, the issues are somewhat different for the lesbian who is going through the "identity confusion" stage at age 18 when identity confusion is more acceptable, than for the lesbian who is going through the "identity confusion" stage at 45 when society expects her not to be confused. In order to plan and provide effective career counseling with lesbian women, career counselors need to be aware of the particular stage of identity development as well as the age of their lesbian clients.

Myers et al. (1991) identified the phases which members of marginalized groups must accomplish on their path to a positive self-identity, which they call the OTAID model (Optimal Theory Applied to Identity Development). Briefly, these phases include: (0) absence of conscious awareness, (1) individuation, (2) dissonance, (3) immersion, (4) internalization, (5) integration, and (6) transformation. In this comprehensive model the authors "provide a unifying system for understanding and conceptualizing the identity development process and describe the effect of oppression on self-identity" (p. 58). Myers et al. (1991) acknowledged the work of Cass (1979) in expanding the scope of identity formation in a multicultural context.

Pope and Jelly (1991) described the "coming out" process as a self-identity process and compared the developmental stages in self-identity formation for gays and lesbians to those of major developmental theorists, including Freud, Erickson, Piaget, Kohlberg, and Super. Elliott (1990) described "coming out" as a unique process which differentiates lesbians and gay men from other minority cultures. Lesbians and gay men are probably the only group where the family of origin has to be informed about their minority membership status. This presents a powerful cohesive experience for gay males and lesbians–a rite of passage.

"Coming out" is an important and necessary developmental task for anyone who is predominantly homosexually-oriented. Pope (1994) identified some of the inherent problems in delayed mastery of such developmental tasks as accepting one's sexual orientation ("coming out") along with the concomitant development of appropriate dating and relationship strategies with same sex partners. This may cause a developmental domino effect which may have long-term and pervasive repercussions for those individuals who come out in their 30s, 40s, 50s, or even later. Coleman, Butcher, and Carson (1984) also gave an explanation of general developmental stages and the tasks associated with each stage. "If developmental tasks are not mastered at the appropriate stage, the individual suffers from immaturities and incompetencies and is placed at a serious disadvantage in adjusting at later developmental levels–that is, the individual becomes increasingly vulnerable through accumulated failures to master psychosocial requirements. . . . Some developmental tasks are set by the individual's own needs, some by the physical and social environment. Members of different socioeconomic and sociocultural groups face somewhat different developmental tasks" (p. 111).

"Coming Out"

> "Coming out" has been defined by Altman (1971) as "the whole process whereby a person comes to identify himself/herself as homosexual, and recognizes his/her position as part of a stigmatized and semi-hidden minority . . . The development of a homosexual identity is a long process that usually begins during adolescence, though sometimes considerably later. Because of the fears and ignorance that surround our views of sex, children discover sexual feelings and behavior

incompletely, and often accompanied by great pangs of guilt
. . . (Many of us) manage to hide into our twenties a full
realization that (we are) not like (them)." (pp. 15-16)

The issue for gay men and lesbian women of "coming out" in
the workplace and in their career has been an important one. From
"how to" (Croteau & Hedstrom, 1993; Pope & Schecter, 1992) to
the "why's" (Brown, 1975; Hetherington, Hillerbrand, & Etringer,
1989; Pope, 1994), this issue has been part of both the professional
and popular literature. The specific practices identified here include
discussing the advantages and disadvantages of coming out in the
workplace and career (Belz, 1993; Brown, 1975; Hetherington, Hillerbrand, & Etringer, 1989; Morgan & Brown, 1991; Pope, 1991;
Pope, Rodriguez, & Chang, 1992), as well as how to go about doing
it (Croteau & Hedstrom, 1993; Elliott, 1993; Pope, 1991; Pope &
Schecter, 1992); special programming for gays and lesbians, which
might include what to include in a resume (Elliott, 1993; Hetherington, Hillerbrand, & Etringer, 1989; Pope, Rodriguez, & Chang,
1992) or what to say or not say on a job interview (Hetherington,
Hillerbrand, & Etringer, 1989; Pope, Rodriguez, & Chang, 1992);
organizing special job fairs (Elliott, 1993; Hetherington, Hillerbrand, & Etringer, 1989) and support groups (Croteau & Hedstrom,
1993; Hetherington, Hillerbrand, & Etringer, 1989); establishing a
special mechanism for conducting informational interviews with
"out" lesbian and gay workers (Belz, 1993; Croteau & Hedstrom,
1993; Hetherington, Hillerbrand, & Etringer, 1989); and providing
special informational interview questions and special job search
questions (Hetherington & Orzek, 1989).

Because few gay males or lesbians can be identified merely by
appearance (Goffman, 1963), the decision to "come out" at work is
an important one for all gay males or lesbians. There are two distinct issues here–(1) reasons to "come out" or not to "come out";
and (2) methods of accomplishing this task.

Pope (1994) has identified many reasons to disclose your sexual
orientation to your coworkers and your company. These include:
individual mental health and full integration of the many aspects
which go into making up each individual person; personal reasons,
such as honesty, integration of your sexuality into other aspects of

your life, recognition of who you are as a person, and support from those around you; professional/political/societal reasons, such as providing a role model for other gay males and lesbians, desensitizing co-workers and oneself toward the issue, and eliminating any fear of blackmail; and practical reasons such as domestic partner benefits, bringing partners to work-sponsored events, and in order to prevent "slips of the tongue" and embarrassment when sexual orientation is disclosed in everyday conversation with coworkers.

There are also important reasons to not "come out" at work. These include: the fear of harassment (either physical or emotional); fear of the effect this disclosure may have on hiring, personnel, and advancement decisions ("glass ceiling"); fear of alienation, isolation, and rejection; fear of being different from the majority culture or of being the same as every member of the minority culture; and fear of the invasion of privacy. These fears, however, may be confronted and discussed with a counselor or a support network of coworkers, supervisors, and peers.

For the gay male or lesbian it may be important to determine if these fears are based on reality, on previous experiences, or on the person's own internalized homophobia. The environment must be objectively observed and analyzed for actual clues to the general corporate/organizational climate [for example, corporate anti-discrimination statement and gay/lesbian employees group, inclusionary or exclusionary language (are only "wives and husbands" invited to corporate events?)], as well as the individual department, manager, or coworkers' attitudes toward sexual orientation issues (for example, types of jokes which are told and tolerated, newspaper articles on the bulletin boards) (Croteau & Hedstrom, 1993; Pope, 1994).

The second issue to be addressed is a practical one of "how to" go about disclosing sexual orientation at work. It is important to conceptualize the process of "coming out" as one having different levels. Further, "coming out" is a continuous process that has no end; gay males and lesbians must make this decision to "come out" any time they meet a new person and in any new situation.

Pope (1994) has identified different ways to "come out" and the issues to be considered as "who, when, where, and how." "Who" includes the decision of whom to tell and may include the person who is conducting the job interview as well as the newly hired person's supervisor, manager, evaluator, peers, or people they supervise. "When" is a decision of timing and may include: on the resume, during your job interview, on the first day of the new job, during the first weeks or months, much later when they get to know the person, or never. "Where" includes the decision to disclose to individuals one at a time or to many people in a group; however, if a group is chosen, then another decision must be made regarding the type of group–subordinate, peer, or supervisory. "How" is a style issue. Some gay males and lesbians are more comfortable with a subtle style while others want to make a strong statement. Methods here may include using the correct gender-specific pronouns when speaking of dates or love relationships, matter of fact statements of reality, or defiant announcements based on homophobic, racist, or sexist comments made in the workplace.

The methods of coming out fall into four general categories: (1) the "American Civil Liberties Union" approach, also known as "the champion of all the oppressed" approach, where the person responds that he or she is offended when any racist, sexist, ageist, or homophobic remark is made by coworkers; (2) the "Rock Hudson/Johnny Mathis" approach where the person is out of the closet in their private life but not out of the closet in their career; (3) the "Martina Navratilova" approach where the person uses the correct pronoun for their partner, date, or lover very matter of factly; and (4) the "Queer Nation" approach where the person announces it publicly by every act they do and has the attitude that it does not matter whether other people accept them or not (Pope, 1994).

Discrimination

As simple as it may seem, talking with a gay or lesbian client openly about issues of employment discrimination is important. Even if the client does not bring it up, the issues ought to be discussed so that the client is aware of both the career counselor's sensitivity and knowledge in this area (Brown, 1975; Croteau & Hedstrom, 1993; Elliott, 1993; Hetherington, Hillerbrand, & Etringer, 1989; Pope, 1991; Pope, Rodriguez, & Chang, 1992). The special practices cited in the literature include talking openly about discrimination against gays and lesbians (Brown, 1975; Croteau & Hedstrom, 1993; Elliott, 1993; Hetherington, Hillerbrand, & Etringer, 1989; Pope, 1991; Pope, Rodriguez, & Chang, 1992); surveying local businesses for information on their employment policies (Elliott, 1993) and getting a copy of their equal employment opportunity (EEO) statements (Elliott, 1993); providing information on geographic location and size of the gay/lesbian community (Belz, 1993; Elliott, 1993; Hetherington, Hillerbrand, & Etringer, 1989); helping clients overcome their own internalized negative stereotypes (homophobia) (Chung & Harmon, in press; Hetherington & Orzek, 1989; Morgan & Brown, 1991; Pope, Rodriguez, & Chang, 1992); helping clients avoid arrest for meeting same sex sexual partners in bars, parks, rest rooms, etc. (Brown, 1975); providing information on local, state, and national laws regarding discrimination on the basis of sexual orientation (Morgan & Brown, 1991); and helping clients construct affirming work environments (Croteau & Hedstrom, 1993).

Occupational Stereotypes and Networking

Employment discrimination is a reality for lesbian and gay male clients. Such discrimination may be both external–such as the attitudes of others that gays and lesbians should not be hired as teachers–and internal–such as the self-attitude that they can only be themselves in "gay dominated" occupations such as–for males–hairdresser, interior decorator, or nurse. This occupational stereotyping is a result of a variety of factors, including physical safety and societal prejudices, and can be self-limiting for the gay male or lesbian woman who fails to challenge these stereotypes. A counterbalance to these stereotypes can be provided by occupational role modeling, where gay and lesbian workers who are successful in occupations which are outside the societal stereotypes are used for panels or informational interviews.

Other special practices include career shadowing of other gay/lesbian workers (Belz, 1993); providing information on national lesbian/gay networks of professional and community people (Belz, 1993; Elliott, 1993; Hetherington & Orzek, 1989); identifying existing gay and lesbian resources in the community (Elliott, 1993; Hetherington, Hillerbrand, & Etringer, 1989; Morgan & Brown, 1991); supporting and encouraging gay/lesbian professionals as role models for students (Chung & Harmon, in press; Elliott, 1993; Hetherington, Hillerbrand, & Etringer, 1989; Morgan & Brown, 1991); internships or cooperative education placements in gay/lesbian owned/operated businesses (Hetherington, Hillerbrand, & Etringer, 1989); and establishing a mentoring program (Elliott, 1993).

Psychological Testing

Special assessment interventions have only recently become important issues in career counseling. The use of career interest inventories, other personality tests, and card sorts are all important interventions in the arsenal of career counselors; how these items are used with lesbian women and gay men is becoming increasingly important. Pope (1992) identified and analyzed the use and misuse of specific subscales on five major psychological inventories used in career counseling and personnel selection (Strong Interest Inventory, Myers-Briggs Type Indicator, Edwards Personal Preference Schedule, California Psychological Inventory, and Minnesota Multiphasic Personality Inventory). Using a case study methodology, Pope wove into the cases technical and psychometric data to illustrate how psychological tests have been misused with gay and lesbian clients.

Pope and Jelly (1991) discussed the use of the Myers-Briggs Type Indicator (MBTI) with gay and lesbian clients. They reported on preliminary data suggesting that not "coming out" for a gay man or lesbian woman may mask a true understanding of self and, therefore, be a source of distortions on self-report inventories like the MBTI, and may lead to changes in self-report inventories after the developmental task of "coming out" is accomplished. Belz (1993) also identified special assessment procedures to be used with gay and lesbian clients such as making new cards in a values card sort, such as, "being out on the job." Chung and Harmon (in press) used the Self-Directed Search (SDS) to compare gay and heterosexual men of equivalent age, socioeconomic background, ethnicity, student status, and education. They found that gay men scored higher on the Artistic and Social scales of the SDS and lower on the Realistic and Investigative scales. They also found that gay men's aspirations were less traditional for men, but that they were not lower in status than the aspirations of the heterosexual men in this study.

Couples and Other Family Issues

Couples counseling with dual career couples or discordant couples (one person is "out," the other is "closeted") (Belz, 1993; Hetherington, Hillerbrand, & Etringer, 1989) is important for the male couple or female couple with no experience and only few "out" dual career couple role models. Hetherington, Hillerbrand, and Etringer (1989) discussed the issues facing men in male dual-career couples–how to present the relationship, how to introduce one's partner, whether to openly acknowledge the lover relationship, and how to deal with social events. Belz (1993) discussed male dual career couple issues as well, including geographic location, lifestyle that partners want to maintain while employed, problems that a job may cause for a partner who may not want to be as open about his or her sexual orientation, when to tell people at work, and how to handle situations which may arise at work which involve a partner.

Advocating for Gay and Lesbian Clients

The career counselor should be gay/lesbian affirmative. This goes beyond the "do no harm" admonition to encompass a positive advocacy for gay and lesbian clients and their rights (Belz, 1993; Brown, 1975; Croteau & Hedstrom, 1993; Hetherington, Hillerbrand, & Etringer, 1989; Hetherington & Orzek, 1989). The two most often mentioned practices include working to change the laws (Brown, 1975; Pope & Schecter, 1992) and working to stop police entrapment of gay men (Brown, 1975; Pope & Schecter, 1992).

CONCLUSION

The purpose of this article was to identify special issues in career development for gays and lesbians. This information may then be used by counselors doing career counseling or instituted as part of an overall career services center when working with lesbian women and gay men. What we want to know, regardless of gender, is whether there are unique counseling practices which are reported in the literature as being used effectively and specifically with gays and lesbians or that are especially useful with this population.

It also must be noted that much of the literature which has been reviewed here is anecdotal and based on clinical observations. As such, it has not yet been reinforced by follow-up quantitative studies. Although this is a weakness of the literature, it does not mean that the recommendations are without value.

The special issues identified here may indeed be representative of the practices of professional career counselors who confront these issues, especially if these interventions are consistently mentioned in the reviewed literature. Hetherington et al. (1989), in fact, reviewed several authors who emphasized that career counseling is one of the most constructive ways that counselors can assist lesbian and gay clients to improve the quality of their lives.

Much research remains to be done on the types of special career counseling practices which are justified for lesbian and gay populations. Special interventions may be warranted for lesbian women separate from gay men, because of the special role of gender in career development (Hansen, 1984). Now that this area of research has become acceptable in academic institutions, the quality and quantity of such research will continue to multiply until we can truly understand what special issues are important for our lesbian and gay clients who are seeking assistance with their careers.

REFERENCES

Altman, D. (1971). *Homosexual: Oppression and liberation.* New York: Avon Books.

Belz, J. R. (1993). Sexual orientation as a factor in career development. *Career Development Quarterly, 41,* 197-200.

Brown, D. A. (1975). Career counseling for the homosexual. In R. D. Burack & R. C. Reardon (Eds.), *Facilitating career development* (pp. 234-247). Springfield, IL: Charles C Thomas.

Buhrke, R. A. (1989). Incorporating lesbian and gay issues into counselor training: A resource guide. *Journal of Counseling and Development, 68,* 77-80.

Buhrke, R. A., Ben-Ezra, L. A., Hurley, M. E., & Ruprecht, L. J. (1992). Content analysis and methodological critique of articles concerning lesbian and gay male issues in counseling journals. *Journal of Counseling Psychology, 39,* 91-99.

Buhrke, R. A., & Douce, L. A. (1991). Training issues for counseling psychologists in working with lesbians and gay men. *Counseling Psychologist, 19,* 216-234.

Cass, V. (1979). Homosexual identity formation: A theoretical model. *Journal of Homosexuality, 4,* 219-235.

Chung, Y. B. (1994). Gay/lesbian career development research: Career decision making and career choice. Paper presented at the national conference of the National Career Development Association, Albuquerque, NM.

Chung, Y. B., & Harmon, L. W. (in press). The career interests and aspirations of gay men: How sex-role orientation is related. *Journal of Vocational Behavior.*

Coleman, J. C., Butcher, J. N., & Carson, R. C. (1984). *Abnormal psychology and modern life* (7th ed.). Glenview, IL: Scott, Foresman and Company.

Croteau, J. M., & Hedstrom, S. M. (1993). Integrating commonality and difference: The key to career counseling with lesbian women and gay men. *Career Development Quarterly, 41,* 201-209.

Diamant, L. (Ed.) (1993). *Homosexual issues in the workplace.* Washington, DC: Taylor & Francis.

Elliott, J. E. (1990). Career development with lesbian and gay clients. Paper presented at the meeting of the American Psychological Association, Boston, MA.

Elliott, J. E. (1993). Career development with lesbian and gay clients. *Career Development Quarterly, 41,* 210-226.

Elliott, J. E. (1993). Lesbian and gay concerns in career development. In L. Diamant (Ed.), *Homosexual issues in the workplace* (pp. 25-44). Washington, DC: Taylor & Francis.

Fassinger, R. E. (1994). Gay/lesbian career development research: Lesbian issues. Paper presented as part of a symposium at the national conference of the National Career Development Association, Albuquerque, NM.

Gelso, C. J., & Fassinger, R. E. (1990). Counseling psychology: Theory and research on interventions. *Annual Review of Psychology, 41,* 355-386.

Goffman, E. (1963). *Stigma: Notes on the management of a spoiled identity.* Englewood Cliffs, NJ: Prentice-Hall.

Gonsiorek, J. C. (1984). Psychotherapeutic issues with gay and lesbian clients. In P. A. Keller & L. G. Ritt (Eds.), *Innovations in clinical practice: A source book* (Volume 3). Sarasota, FL: Professional Resources Exchange.

Hansen, J. C. (1984). *User's guide to the SVIB.* Palo Alto, CA: Consulting Psychologists Press.

Hetherington, C., Hillerbrand, E., & Etringer, B. (1989). Career counseling with gay men: Issues and recommendations for research. *Journal of Counseling and Development, 67,* 452-454.

Hetherington, D., & Orzek, A. M. (1989). Career counseling and life planning with lesbian women. *Journal of Counseling and Development, 68,* 52-57.

Morgan, K. S., & Brown, L. S. (1991). Lesbian career development, work behavior, and vocational counseling. *Counseling Psychologist, 19,* 273-291.

Myers, L. J., Speight, S. L., Highlen, P. S., Cox, C. I., Reynolds, A. L., Adams, E. M., & Hanley, C. P. (1991). Identity development and worldview: Toward an optimal conceptualization. *Journal of Counseling and Development, 70,* 54-63.

Orzek, A. M. (1992). Career counseling for the gay and lesbian community. In S. Dworkin & F. Gutierrez (Eds.), *Counseling gay men and lesbians: Journey to the end of the rainbow* (pp. 23-34). Alexandria, VA: American Counseling Association.

Index

© 1996 by The Haworth Press, Inc. All rights reserved.

Haworth
DOCUMENT DELIVERY
SERVICE

This valuable service provides a single-article order form for any article from a Haworth journal.

- *Time Saving:* No running around from library to library to find a specific article.
- *Cost Effective:* All costs are kept down to a minimum.
- *Fast Delivery:* Choose from several options, including same-day FAX.
- *No Copyright Hassles:* You will be supplied by the original publisher.
- *Easy Payment:* Choose from several easy payment methods.

Open Accounts Welcome for...
- Library Interlibrary Loan Departments
- Library Network/Consortia Wishing to Provide Single-Article Services
- Indexing/Abstracting Services with Single Article Provision Services
- Document Provision Brokers and Freelance Information Service Providers

---

MAIL or *FAX* THIS ENTIRE ORDER FORM TO:

Haworth Document Delivery Service
The Haworth Press, Inc.
10 Alice Street
Binghamton, NY 13904-1580

or FAX: 1-800-895-0582
or CALL: 1-800-342-9678
9am-5pm EST

PLEASE SEND ME PHOTOCOPIES OF THE FOLLOWING SINGLE ARTICLES:
1) Journal Title: _____
  Vol/Issue/Year:_____Starting & Ending Pages:_____
  Article Title:_____
_____

2) Journal Title: _____
  Vol/Issue/Year:_____Starting & Ending Pages:_____
  Article Title:_____
_____

3) Journal Title: _____
  Vol/Issue/Year:_____Starting & Ending Pages:_____
  Article Title:_____
_____

4) Journal Title: _____
  Vol/Issue/Year:_____Starting & Ending Pages:_____
  Article Title:_____
_____

(See other side for Costs and Payment Information)

COSTS: Please figure your cost to order quality copies of an article.
1. Set-up charge per article: $8.00
   ($8.00 × number of separate articles) _____
2. Photocopying charge for each article:
   1-10 pages: $1.00 _____

   11-19 pages: $3.00 _____

   20-29 pages: $5.00 _____

   30+ pages: $2.00/10 pages _____
3. Flexicover (optional): $2.00/article _____
4. Postage & Handling: US: $1.00 for the first article/
   $.50 each additional article _____

   Federal Express: $25.00 _____

   Outside US: $2.00 for first article/
   $.50 each additional article _____
5. Same-day FAX service: $.35 per page _____

   GRAND TOTAL: _____

_____

METHOD OF PAYMENT: (please check one)
❑ Check enclosed   ❑ Please ship and bill. PO # _____
   (sorry we can ship and bill to bookstores only! All others must pre-pay)
❑ Charge to my credit card: ❑ Visa; ❑ MasterCard; ❑ Discover;
   ❑ American Express;

Account Number: _____   Expiration date: _____

Signature: *X*_____

Name: _____   Institution: _____

Address: _____

_____

City: _____   State: _____   Zip: _____

Phone Number: _____   FAX Number: _____

_____

MAIL or *FAX* THIS ENTIRE ORDER FORM TO:

Haworth Document Delivery Service | **or FAX:** 1-800-895-0582
The Haworth Press, Inc. | **or CALL:** 1-800-342-9678
10 Alice Street | 9am-5pm EST)
Binghamton, NY 13904-1580 |

DATE DUE

MAY 15 1998	
NOV 15 1998	

DEMCO, INC. 38-2931